The
ODDITORIUM

**David Bramwell
& Jo Keeling**

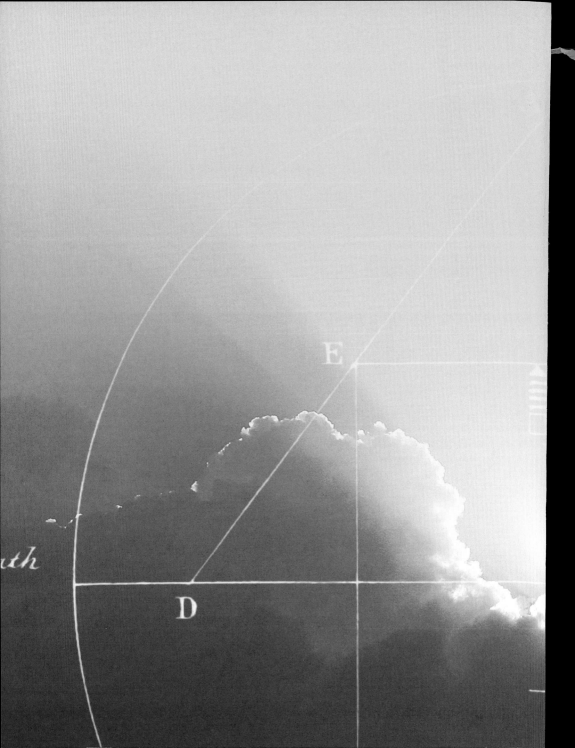

The ODDITORIUM

The tricksters, eccentrics, deviants and inventors whose obsessions changed the world

David Bramwell
& Jo Keeling

BREWER'S

First published in Great Britain in 2016 by Brewer's, an imprint of
Chambers Publishing Ltd. An Hachette UK company.
Brewer's® is a registered trademark of Chambers Publishing Ltd.
Copyright © David Bramwell and Jo Keeling

British Library Cataloguing in Publication Data: a catalogue record
for this title is available from the British Library.
Library of Congress Catalog Card Number: on file.
Hardback: 978 1 4736 4031 3
eBook: 978 1 4736 4150 1

4

The publisher has used its best endeavours to ensure that any website addresses referred
to in this book are correct and active at the time of going to press. However, the publisher
and the author have no responsibility for the websites and can make no guarantee that a
site will remain live or that the content will remain relevant, decent or appropriate.
The publisher has made every effort to mark as such all words which it believes to be
trademarks. The publisher should also like to make it clear that the presence of a word in the
book, whether marked or unmarked, in no way affects its legal status as a trademark.
Every reasonable effort has been made by the publisher to trace the copyright holders of
material in this book. Any errors or omissions should be notified in writing to the publisher,
who will endeavour to rectify the situation for any reprints and future editions.
Printed and bound in Great Britian, by CPI Group (UK) Ltd.

Chambers Publishing Ltd policy is to use papers that are natural, renewable and recyclable
products and made from wood grown in sustainable forests. The logging and manufacturing
processes are expected to conform to the environmental regulations of the country of origin.

Carmelite House
50 Victoria Embankment
London EC4Y 0DZ
www.chambers.co.uk

Editor: Jo Keeling
Art director: Tina Smith
Designer: Johnathan Montelongo
Sub editor: Dave Perrett

CONTENTS

1 TRICKSTERS & SUBVERSIVES

2 CREATIVE MAVERICKS

3 WILD AT HEART

4 PIONEERS & INVENTORS

5 EXPLORERS OF THE MIND

'Originality is unexplored territory. You get there by carrying a canoe. You can't take a taxi.'
–Alan Alda

FOREWORD *by John Mitchinson*

In 1931, in the remote Cornish parish of Warleggan, a new vicar took over as rector of St Bartholomew's. Reverend Frederick Densham's arrival and tenure is still talked about in the West Country. With single-minded determination, the new vicar set about implementing a regime which quickly alienated his congregation. He banned whist drives and music and preached the virtues of vegetarianism to a community of farmers. The final straw came when he painted the inside of his ancient church with garish red and blue stripes. As his congregation deserted him, Densham gradually filled his church with cardboard cutouts and name cards and continued to take services, preaching sermons to his quiet but attentive paper flock. He died there 22 years later, having subsisted on a diet composed mostly of nettles and porridge.

Before you scour the pages that follow, Reverend Densham's story is not among the exemplary lives that David Bramwell and Jo Keeling have gathered here. In the end, his story doesn't quite have the detail and texture that makes *The Odditorium* so remarkable and useful. Densham was certainly an eccentric, but this book is much more than a catalogue of eccentrics. All we know is that he did his own thing. The reasons why he did it are lost with him.

Outside Cornwall, his memory survives through the mad vicar in Daphne du Maurier's *Jamaica Inn*, which was modeled on him and the performance of Edward Woodward who played Densham in 2009's *A Congregation of Ghosts*. What Densham's story does do is reflect the theme that connects all the stories that follow. That theme is obsession. You are about to spend some gloriously happy hours in the company of visionaries, rogues, mystics, pioneers, charlatans, mountebanks, geniuses and clowns, all of them in the grip of something they felt that was bigger and more important than their own life and destiny.

In our post-Freudian world it is fashionable to view obsession in an overwhelmingly negative light: a psychologist, we feel sure, would have plenty to say about Densham's odd behaviour. Which is why this book is as important as it is entertaining. Each life featured is a reminder that breakthroughs in thought, science, art and social organization are rarely the product of rational thought and meetings. They are the bastard children of obsession.

As so often the clue is in the deep history of the word itself. 'Obsess' literally means 'to sit opposite', from *ob* 'against' and *sedere* 'sit'. This gradually grew into the idea of a siege – 'there's something over there that I want or need' – which in turn darkens into the idea of being haunted. Obsession is what takes us to extremes; it leads us out of our comfort zone. While it can lead to madness, isolation, anti-social behaviour and financial ruin, it is also what allows us to discover the new and the original: it is the path that leads us to the future. It's only from the edges that we can see the shape and size of the whole.

So, treat this book's rich and subversive content as a series of signposts to our own road less travelled. Each story within it, however unlikely, reminds us that there are no limits and no rules when it comes to human potential. Even Densham's sad story carries a challenge. Despite the loneliness and the diet of nettles and porridge, who would you rather be – the mad vicar preaching with conviction to his ideal congregation or the nameless parishioners who abandoned him? At the end of Woody Allen's *Annie Hall* the narrator tells a story which seems to sum this up perfectly: 'A guy walks into a psychiatrist's office and says, "Hey doc, my brother's crazy! He thinks he's a chicken." Then the doc says, "Why don't you turn him in?" Then the guy says, "I would, but I need the eggs."'

We all need the eggs and this book reminds us why.

John Mitchinson was the first QI researcher and has co-written all ten of the QI books, including *The QI Book of the Dead*. He is also co-founder of the crowd-funding publisher Unbound.

'Welcome seekers!'

These were the opening words that maverick producer Ken Campbell used to greet his audiences, shortly before unveiling another of his epic and fantastical theatre productions. Campbell's singular approach to theatre led to ground-breaking shows, such as the 24-hour long *Warp* (1979), a prank on the Royal Shakespeare Company that led to a Scotland Yard investigation and a version of *Macbeth* (2001) performed entirely in pidgin English, using only didgeridoos for props. Campbell was never happier than when trying to do something that others deemed impossible.

Such was his extraordinary nature that Campbell was often described as mad, to which he would furrow his shagpile eyebrows and retort: 'I'm not mad, I'm just read different books.' For him, 'seeking' was a way of life – a willingness to take a path that was often at odds with the world around him.

The Odditorium is a book for – and about – seekers. It is a celebration of 48 compelling individuals who were driven by obsession, curiosity, trickery, courage and gumption. Along the way, you'll enter the remarkable world of a Victorian prankster who sent 30,000 singular objects through the Royal Mail (including himself and his Irish terrier, Bob); a visionary responsible for creating the world's largest underground temple; a housewife who grew giant peanuts using atomic energy and a man who made it his life's mission to eat every living creature and catalogue their flavours with a palatability chart.

The people featured in this book, however, are not merely celebrated for their eccentricity. In challenging the status quo, many faced persecution, social exclusion and imprisonment. One such was Wilhelm Reich, who advocated a sexual revolution 40 years before the slogan 'make love not war' became a rallying cry of 60s counter-culture. Others had to deal with ostracisation, such as Quentin Crisp who stepped out as a flamboyant gay man into a hostile London in the late 1920s, unwilling to compromise his attire or sexuality for society.

'Make no effort to join society. Stay right where you are and wait for society to form around you. Because it most certainly will,' he reasoned (*An Englishman in New York*, 2009). And it did. Politics, war and empires may shape our history, but it is single-minded individuals such as Crisp who help instigate momentous cultural leaps and allow us to make sense of our ever-changing world. For every Joseph Stalin there is a Rosa Parks.

Like Parks, many of the people featured in *The Odditorium* came from humble backgrounds. You'll enter the lives of outsider artists, pioneering linguists, atomic scientists, time travellers, S&M practitioners and sculptors of mind-boggling architecture. And with the exception of the odd Victorian polymath and a Cambridge-educated occultist, many of them also happened to have been housewives, teachers, travelling salesmen, an unemployed plumber or a blind street musician. Each story is testament to the idea that following our passions – no matter how at odds with society – can transform our lives and the lives of those around us.

The Odditorium also unearths a number of remarkable but little-known women's stories – a baroness now credited with creating the most important work of art in the 20th century; a 'social pariah' who published a communist manifesto five years before Marx and Engels; and a 'housewife from Wales' dismissed by critics as a 'feminist with an axe to grind,' who spent her life championing a radical theory of evolution, which was eventually taken up by Sir David Attenborough.

Finally, we journey into the lives of pioneers whose visions merely seemed like a good idea at the time – a reminder that we often need a measure of hindsight to judge a life. Thomas Midgley Junior's inventions had a devastating effect on the planet, while Russian author Ayn Rand created a philosophy – still popular with slices of society in the US – that justifies selfishness as a principle aim in life.

Each chapter of *The Odditorium* ends with a seekers' directory: recommended reading, podcasts and documentaries, as well as pilgrimages and field trips so you further explore the lives of these singular characters. There are even practical exercises you can try at home, such as how to experiment with time and shake yourself free of your 'reality tunnel'. It only remains for us to end as we begun: welcome seekers! DB & JK

1 & 3

TRICKSTERS & SUBVERSIVES

1

TRICKSTERS& SUBVERSIVES

Every year in Cumbria, the Santon Bridge Inn hosts
the World's Biggest Liar competition in which contestants
take to the stage to spin the most ridiculous but convincing
yarn. The coveted title of 'Biggest Liar in the World' is
currently held by seven-times winner Johnny 'the liar' Graham
who, among other things, claims to pilot an underwater
wheelie bin. This competition is a gathering of tricksters –
snake-oil sellers with silver tongues.

In myth and art, the trickster can be found in every culture
across the globe, whether in the guise of Loki, Reynard the
Fox, Roald Dahl's Matilda, Wile E. Coyote or Bart Simpson.
It is the trickster who whispers in our ears when we feel

the urge to pull a prank, heckle, tell a whopping great lie or spread a little chaos. But chaos – as science has taught us – also has the power to bring the world into order. Mercurial, contrary and cunning, tricksters are the embodiment of a paradox; they are the necessary grit in the oyster, as essential to society as the mores and rules they delight in subverting.

Some people are just born to make mischief. This chapter celebrates a remarkable collection of individuals who fooled the world through their lies, forgeries, antics and parlour tricks. Meet Cyril Hoskin, a Devonian plumber's son who successfully passed himself off as a Tibetan lama; political prankster Screaming Lord Sutch; and the self-proclaimed Emperor of the United States, who drew a crowd of 30,000 to his funeral in San Francisco.

For some, it takes one visit from the trickster to change the world for ever – such as Kate and Maggie Fox, whose prank inadvertently paved the way for a global spiritualist movement. It seems that other folk – such as Reginald Bray, who posted 30,000 singular objects through the Royal Mail, or performer Ken Campbell, whose RSC hoax led to a Scotland Yard investigation – can only truly be happy when planning the next 'great caper'.

CORGI

T. LOBSANG RAMPA
THE THIRD EYE

TUESDAY LOBSANG RAMPA

The Devonian lama

Picture if you can, post-war Britain circa 1956. The country is undergoing great social and cultural change. The Suez Crisis has marked the final death knell for the British Empire and a young English writer, Colin Wilson, has became an overnight sensation with his book *The Outsider* – putting a more positive spin on the French philosophy of existentialism. In a spirit of optimism and self-enquiry, a new generation is turning away from Christianity and post-Victorian mores and opening up to Kerouac's Beat Generation, Sartre and Zen. They hang out in espresso bars, discuss philosophy, listen to jazz and are intrigued by the exoticism and wisdom of the East. It is the perfect time for the publication of a book called *The Third Eye*.

Written by Dr Tuesday Lobsang Rampa, *The Third Eye* is an autobiographical account of a wealthy Tibetan growing up in Lhasa where, at the age of seven, he is sent to a lamasery to study Buddhism. The book is full of extraordinary stories of his early life there. Rampa recounts how he achieved psychic powers after a painful trepanning operation to open up the 'third eye' in his forehead. Elsewhere, there are first-hand accounts of levitation, clairvoyance, meetings with the Dalai Lama and even an encounter with the Abominable Snowman:

'We looked at each other, both of us frozen with fright for a period which seemed ageless. It was pointing a hand at me and making a curious mewing noise like a kitten. The head had no frontal lobes but seemed to slope back almost directly from the heavy brows. The chin receded greatly and the teeth were large and prominent. As I looked and perhaps jumped with fright, the yeti screeched, turned and leaped away.'
–Lobsang Rampa, *The Third Eye* (1956)

At first Rampa's publisher, Secker & Warburg, was not entirely convinced by the authenticity of *The Third Eye*.

During an early meeting Rampa's editor, who had learned a smattering of Tibetan, greeted the author with a friendly, 'Hello, how are you?' in his native tongue. The welcome was met with silence. When informed that he had been addressed in Tibetan, Rampa collapsed to the floor and began to scream in agony. Finally climbing back on to his chair, he explained that before leaving Tibet he had put a curse on himself to no longer understand or speak Tibetan, for fear of 'giving away his secrets', (forgetting, perhaps, that he had just presented his publisher with a book full of them). In actual fact, Rampa only spoke English with a curiously strong West Country burr.

Undeterred, Secker & Warburg published *The Third Eye*. It sold a third of a million copies in the first two years in the UK alone – and was soon found in every bookshop, airport and kiosk across the West. The *Times Literary Supplement* (1956) wrote: '*The Third Eye* comes near to being a work of art.'

AN AUSPICIOUS OWL-SPOTTING ACCIDENT

While *The Third Eye* continued to sell phenomenally well, Rampa had a number of detractors, notably the Tibetologist Heinrich Harrer. Certain that the book was the work of a fraud, Harrer went to the extent of hiring a private detective, Clifford Burgess, to determine the validity of Rampa's book.

What Burgess uncovered surprised even his employer. Not only had Rampa never been to Tibet, he didn't even own a passport. He was, instead, an unemployed plumber's son named Cyril Hoskin from Plympton in Devon. After falling out of a tree while owl-spotting one afternoon, Hoskin had put his back out and was unable to work. Wiling away the hours during his convalescence, Hoskin had, it appeared, settled on a drastic career change.

While the press had a field day with Burgess's revelations, Hoskin was unrepentant. In another interview he cheerfully admitted he'd never actually been to Tibet but had acquired his knowledge owing to the fact that he was possessed by the *spirit* of a lama. The story now went that during that fateful afternoon in 1956, while Hoskin was lying at the bottom of a tree half-strangled by his binoculars, an elderly lama was passing by on the astral plane and the pair agreed to swap bodies. Whether at the same time in Tibet a lama was claiming to be a West Country plumber and writing books on how to install a boiler remains, as yet, unverified.

While Rampa lost a few readers after the revelation, he went on to write further adventures in *Doctor from Lhasa* (1959) and *The Rampa Story* (1960), in which he candidly described his years in a Japanese prisoner of war camp, his escape by boat to Korea, his arrest and torture in Russia and subsequent getaway to Europe masquerading as a luxury car salesman.

After this, there was no stopping him. *Cave of the Ancients* (1963) tells of a highly advanced race who once lived underground, *My Visit to Venus* (1957) describes his encounters with Venusians, *You Forever* (1965) is a manual for developing psychic powers and *The Saffron Robe* (1966) describes his meetings with the Dalai Lama.

These were followed by more books, a meditation album (delivered in a West Country lilt) and perhaps his finest achievement, *Living with the Lama* (1964), a book that he claimed was dictated to him by his cat, Mrs Fifi Greywhiskers.

In our current age, it is almost impossible to imagine that another Tuesday Lobsang Rampa could ever get as far as making it into print. While avatars and social networking profiles allow us to present the world with a myriad of alter egos, it is much harder to keep secrets. Cyril Hoskin lived in a pre-Internet age, one before budget flights opened up parts of the world that had hitherto been unknown to the West.

Like **Carlos Castaneda**, Rampa spun tales of worlds and people that many desperately wanted to believe existed. Understanding our inherent fascination with monsters and magic, Hoskin was playing to the crowd. We may be older and wiser now, but are we the happier for knowing that things like the Loch Ness monster don't exist?

With the exception of a Dutchman who tried to emulate Rampa by opening his third eye with a power drill, Hoskin's body of work can still be viewed as a power for good. *The Third Eye* generated unprecedented interest in Tibet in

In the 1960s and 1970s, Carlos Castaneda wrote a number of books that purported to be autobiographical accounts of his mystical training with a Mexican shaman, Don Juan Matus. They were later discredited by experts.

19

the 20th century; many leading scholars in Tibetology admit that it was Rampa who set them on their paths. And while the Dalai Lama has repeatedly denied ever meeting Rampa – describing his books as 'highly imaginative works of fiction' – he has also stated that Rampa raised public awareness of the plight of Tibet.

Like Joshua Norton, who proclaimed himself to be the Emperor of America, there is little doubt that Hoskin really did come to believe he was a Tibetan Lama. He died in 1981, still swearing that 'everything in my books is true'. Whatever plane of existence he may inhabit now, Hoskin would be heartened to know that *The Third Eye* remains to this day one of the world's best-selling books on Tibetan Buddhism. DB

HARRY BENSLEY

The other man in the iron mask

In the winter of 1908, a strange act appeared in the music halls of south-east England. Sandwiched between comedians and performing midgets, he gave his name only as 'The Man in the Iron Mask'. Face covered by a knight's helmet, he explained that, because of a bet, he was seeing whether it was possible to walk around the world without being identified.

That simple wager had been complicated with a list of other conditions. He had to remain masked throughout the journey, to visit every county in England (getting a signature from a mayor or other dignitary), to keep himself alive only by selling postcards and souvenirs, and to never accept any gifts from strangers. According to the *Brighton Herald*'s article in February of that year, 'perhaps the most extraordinary condition of all is that he should find a wife on the road, who must be "between the ages of twenty-five and thirty, well-educated, of even temper, with some knowledge of music".' The number of conditions on the bet was fiendish – this is the sort of thing that ruins people's lives.

Harry Bensley, the man who seems to have been under the mask, died in 1958 but the legend of this walk around the world has grown. Most accounts start with **a bet between Hugh Cecil Lowther Lonsdale and American millionaire John Morgan**.

Bensley set out from Trafalgar Square on New Year's Day 1908, wearing the 4-pound 6-ounce (2kg) helmet. In Bexleyheath he was arrested for selling goods without a hawker's licence. It looked as if the challenge might be over before he had even left Great Britain. Fortunately, he was allowed to remain masked while in court, giving his name only as 'The Man in the Iron Mask'.

Most retellings of Bensley's story feature the same ending.

Lonsdale said that it would be possible for a man to walk around the world without being identified. Morgan said it couldn't be done – and put his money where his mouth was, offering $100,000 to the person who could complete the challenge. It would be rude not to give it a try.

After trekking across England, America, China, India, Turkey and the Balkans, he reached Genoa in Italy on 14 August 1914, where something terrible happened. Hundreds of miles away in Sarajevo, Archduke Franz Ferdinand of Austria had been assassinated. With war breaking out, Harry was sent a telegram announcing that the bet was off. He would receive only £4,000 to make up for the cancellation of the contest. He removed the mask and threw it to the side of the road. Returning to England, Bensley gave his compensation to charity and signed up for the army.

Despite the length of Bensley's travels, his travels around the world are surprisingly little attested – particularly given the awkward discussions that must have occurred at ports and border crossings. He definitely travelled throughout England, and **the postcards he sold often come up for sale online**. Bensley is in sweater and slacks, one hand in his pocket, looking nonchalant – other than the massive visored helmet covering his head. In front of him is a pram, a sign by his side announcing '£21,000, The Biggest Wager on Record'.

On his travels, he was interviewed by newspapers. A journalist in Brighton described the strangeness of interviewing a masked man, but asserted that he was 'a well-spoken gentleman, evidently of education'. Bensley revealed in interviews that he was not allowed to receive any goods without paying for them, and that the companion travelling with him was a friend, whose keep was paid for out of the iron mask's earnings.

THE PLOT THICKENS AND THE MASK DISAPPEARS
Harry Bensley spent his last years in Brighton, finally dying aged 79 in a house in Riley Road on 21 May 1958. An article written on his death revealed a few more details of his adventures: 'He received marriage offers from 200 women, in England, Australia and America… Instead he married a Manchester pianist, a girl named Kate.' There is a tantalizing reference to the mask, saying that it was stored along with the pram, but that his wife had no idea where they were.

Maybe the answer comes in a feature titled 'The Great Masked Man Hoax Issue' in 1908 of *Answers Weekly*. Published at the end of 1908, the article has a first-person account that

Bensley's family are creating an online archive at mcnaught. orpheusweb. co.uk, which offers a fascinating insight into his journey. Looking at the postcards in order, it seems that Bensley may have changed his helmet somewhere along the way.

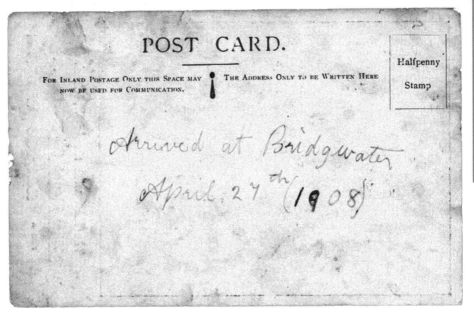

provides a different version of events. The interviewee, who one assumes is Bensley, explains how he was in prison for a minor offence. While there, he tried to figure out what to do for a living, since he had no trade to fall back on. Seeing a copy of the Alexandre Dumas novel *The Vicomte de Bragelonne: Ten Years Later*, he was inspired with the idea of a bogus wager. In **the tell-all article**, the interviewee claims that he walked 2,400 miles in ten months while selling postcards around the country. He says that he supported his journey 'entirely from the sale of my cards and pamphlets, and that I have received nothing in the shape of charity from the first day of my itinerary'.

It looks as if the story of Bensley's adventure survived this early confession. It also survived the obvious fact that John Morgan, the man who made the bet, died in 1913 so could not have sent a telegram ending the bet. While it's easy to gain fame from great feats of exploration, it's even more remarkable to gain such fame without leaving one's home country. *jB*

Yet another version of events claims that Bensley gambled away his inheritance one night during a boozy card game with his friends Morgan and Lonsdale. To save face, Bensley pleaded with them to think of an alternative forfeit; to walk round the world in a mask and find a wife was their harsh challenge.

JOE ORTON

*The playwright incarcerated for
crimes against library books*

In the mid-1960s, a new *enfant terrible* entered the world of theatre: Joe Orton. After the success of his first play on BBC radio, Orton shot to fame with *Entertaining Mr Sloane* (1964) and *Loot* (1965) – scandalizing and delighting audiences with his black comedies, which were laced with caustic wit, moral ambiguity, violence and sexual frisson.

To the outside world, Orton was an overnight success but, like most artists, he'd had his time in the wilderness. For the past eight years, he had shared a tiny one-bed flat in Islington with Kenneth Halliwell, his lover of 16 years. Together, the pair had tried their hands at acting and novel writing, to no avail. The breakthrough finally came – for Orton at least – in the most unlikely form, a six-month prison sentence for crimes against library books.

Orton and Halliwell, openly gay at a time when homosexuality was illegal, shared a contrary streak. In protest against the 'rubbish' that was available in their local library, they began to indulge in a little guerrilla art. Smuggling out piles of books in a satchel, the pair took them home to be given a makeover. Using razor blades, glue and a choice selection of images carefully cut from magazines, they created new covers for the books – sometimes replacing the jacket text with their own and, occasionally, tampering with the text within the books.

A book on exotic caged birds was returned with a cover featuring monkeys on perches; a chimp's face peered from the centre of a flower on the cover of a book on roses; Agatha Christie's *The Secret of Chimneys* featured a giant marauding moggy and the collected plays of Emlyn Williams appeared to include *Knickers Must Fall, He Was Born Grey* and *Fucked by Monty*.

Orton and Halliwell took great delight in returning the books discreetly to the shelves and then hanging around to witness the reactions of anyone selecting their handiwork. As they continued, their prank became more sexual, dark and surreal. Giant animals, wrestling men and nudes began to feature heavily on the covers, while the central image of a biography of the poet John Betjeman was replaced with a man in underpants covered from head to toe in tattoos.

As all the library books were sealed within see-through plastic covers, Halliwell and Orton found they could reverse the wings of the book jacket to reveal the blank side. Here they would type their own synopsis, glue it back and reseal the altered blurb inside the plastic cover. One synopsis of a thriller ended with the line:

'This is one of the most enthralling stories ever written by Miss Sayers. Read this behind closed doors. And have a good shit whilst reading it.'

The staff at Islington Library were largely unimpressed, describing the defaced books as an 'attack by predators'. With Halliwell and Orton as number-one suspects, the head of the library needed proof of their typewriter style and wrote to Halliwell accusing him of being the owner of

THE
GREAT
TUDORS

C. H. Williams · A. F. Pollard · E. P. Cheyney · Douglas Woodruff

R. W. Chambers · A. W. Reed · David Mathew

M. St. Clare Byrne · R. Ellis Roberts · Harold Child

G. B. Harrison · M. T. Stead · C. Read · Alfred Noyes

Hugh Ross Williamson · Hilaire Belloc · W. L. Renwick

Christopher Morris · A. W. Pollard · J. Dover Wilson

EDITED BY KATHARINE GARVIN

an illegally parked car. Halliwell wrote back to proclaim his innocence, ending with 'yours contemptuously, Kenneth L Halliwell', unwittingly supplying the library with the evidence they needed.

The pair got six months in prison. It was a harsh sentence, considering the nature of the crime, and most likely imposed because of their sexuality. Halliwell, who suffered from depression, tried to commit suicide twice. Orton, however, later described his time in prison as 'marvellous'. It had, he claimed, confirmed his suspicion that 'society was rotten' and fuelled his writing.

Not long after the pair's release, Joe had his first success with *The Ruffian on the Stair*. *Entertaining Mr Sloane* and *Loot* followed, to phenomenal critical acclaim. Having become hot property, Orton was asked to write a script for a mooted third Beatles film. His response was *Up Against It*, which featured the loveable mop-tops in scenarios of adultery, homosexuality, cross-dressing and murder, together with a cast of characters that included a dominatrix and gang of anarchists. In one scene, Ringo disrupts a funeral procession with a monologue in praise of debauchery and perversion. To no one's surprise, Orton's included, the script was rejected.

Joe Orton's life ended abruptly in 1967 when he was bludgeoned to death by Halliwell in their bedsit. Halliwell's depression, tranquillizer misuse and growing jealousy had driven him to murder the one person in the world who cared for him. He took an overdose immediately after and died before his lover.

We can only imagine the plays, novels and film scripts that Orton would have produced had his life not been cut short. Were he still alive, he would doubtless have enjoyed the great irony that the vandalized library books, which helped act as a catalyst for his brief but brilliant career, are now displayed as prized works of art in the Islington Local History Centre. DB

JOSHUA NORTON

The Emperor of America

'Everybody understands Mickey Mouse. Few understand
Hermann Hesse. Hardly anyone understands Einstein.
And nobody understands Emperor Norton.'
–Greg Hill, *Principia Discordia* (1979)

On 17 September 1859, London-born Joshua Abraham Norton
declared himself Emperor of the United States of America. He
did this through means of a letter to his local San Francisco
newspaper. 'I accept this title at the peremptory request and
desire of a large majority of the citizens of these United States,'

he explained, before signing the letter 'NORTON I, Emperor of the United States'.

The only official recognition that Emperor Norton received was the 1870 US Census, which listed his occupation as 'emperor' but also noted that he was a lunatic. Nevertheless, the people of San Francisco took him to heart, and he quickly became a well-known and much-loved member of the community.

Norton dressed in a blue military uniform with gold epaulettes, a peacock feather in his hat and an imperial sword on his belt. He was allowed to eat without payment at the finest restaurants, travelled for free on municipal transport and a box was kept for him at San Francisco theatres.

Despite being penniless he began printing his own currency, which was accepted in many of the bars he used to frequent. All this was good for trade. Tourists travelled great distances to San Francisco hoping to glimpse the famous emperor, especially after the opening of the railways.

Norton issued many imperial proclamations. He called for the abolishment of the Democrat and Republican parties, and declared that anyone who referred to San Francisco as 'Frisco' would be subject to a $25 fine.

'Whoever after due and proper warning shall be heard to utter the abominable word "Frisco," which has no linguistic or other warrant, shall be deemed guilty of a High Misdemeanor, and shall pay into the Imperial Treasury as penalty the sum of twenty-five dollars.'
–Emperor Norton, Proclamation of 1872

He cared deeply about the plight of his fellow Americans and campaigned for equal treatment of Native Americans, African-Americans, Chinese and other minorities.

It would not appear to be the case that Norton adopted the title of Emperor in order to gain notoriety or food. He genuinely believed that he was the American Emperor, regardless of what the US constitution said, and so had no choice but to live each day as an emperor would.

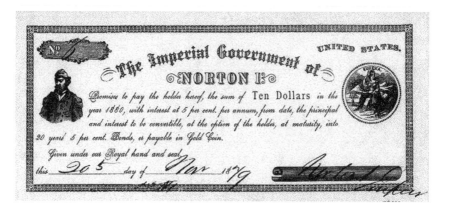

After he died, the city's flags flew at half-mast. His funeral procession was two miles (3.2km) long and contained an estimated 30,000 people – or, to put it another way, pretty much the entire population of the city at the time. Norton's still remains the largest funeral San Francisco has ever seen. He has not been forgotten in that city; there has even been a campaign to rename San Francisco's Oakland Bridge as Emperor Norton Bridge.

Ex-London mayoral candidate Lisa Lovebucket travelled to San Francisco in 2016 to visit his grave on the 198th anniversary of his birth. As she remarked:

'Norton has often been portrayed as a villain or a fool, but he was neither of those. He was a hero. Norton was a living fairy tale, like an American Robin Hood. When children came up to him on the street he would take them into a sweet shop and demand, as Emperor, that they be given sweets. Imagine what a figure like that would look like to the children. There's no mystery, I think, as to why the people loved him so much.'

W REGINALD BRAY

The Picasso of postal art

In 2003, a £10,000 prize was created for any artist in the
UK who could come up with 'an original idea'. Originality, it
seemed, was in short supply and worthy of financial support.
The prize money was put up by author Charles Webb, best
known for *The Graduate* (1963), and his wife, known simply as
Fred. This cash was not offered lightly. Despite the global success
of *The Graduate* as a book, movie and play, money rather than
originality had been in short supply for much of Webbs' lives.

Back in the 1960s, Charles' non-conformism led to his
refusing an inheritance, giving away four houses and selling his
film rights for a small, one-off fee. His happiest moment, he
once confessed in a newspaper interview, was when one of his
sons cooked and ate a copy of the paperback of *The Graduate*
with cranberry sauce. By the end of the 20th century, Charles
and Fred were renting a small apartment above a pet shop in
Sussex and finding it hard to cover the rent. Having returned
to writing, however, after a 20-year hiatus, Webb had received
significant recompense for a new book and film spin-off and
used some of this money to create the prize.

It was eventually awarded to Dan Shelton, a performance
artist living in Brighton. Like Rowan Atkinson's mime artist on
Not the Nine O'Clock News, Shelton's motto was 'My body is my
tool'. Shelton reasoned that, if his body was his art, to protect it
from rights infringement he'd need to copyright his physical self.
Knowing that writers, traditionally, would copyright their work
by sending manuscripts to themselves by registered post, Shelton
figured that he could copyright his art by mailing himself to
himself. It was this original idea that won him the prize.

In preparation for the big day, Shelton used some of the
money to build a special crate, complete with a chair and

Portaloo. Unfortunately, when he approached the Royal Mail, Shelton was told that it was over their allotted weight limit. He decided instead to courier himself to the Tate Modern to see if the gallery would accept him as a piece of art. He did. And, no, they wouldn't. (He'd paid in advance for return delivery to Brighton, just in case.)

'As modern art, it had the stamp of originality,' wrote Jack Malvern in *The Times* the following day, in a feature entitled 'The Artist Who Sent Himself Up' (2002). But was Malvern right? Time to travel back 100 years or so and introduce you to the hero of this feature, W. Reginald Bray.

THE PRANKSTER OF FOREST HILL

Born in 1879 in Forest Hill, south London, Bray grew up to be an upright, middle-class Victorian. He trained to become an accountant – a job he would do for the whole of his life – and enjoyed hobbies typical for a man of his time, namely cycling, stamp-collecting and pubs. He also loved sending postcards and had a keen eye for the ladies.

Bray, however, didn't do things by halves. An obsessive collector of ephemera, by his late teens he was already becoming a leading authority on postmarks, which he also collected in the thousands and carefully catalogued. When his family moved to Devonshire Road in Forest Hill in 1899, the location of their new house may well have been a defining moment in Bray's life. A hundred yards from their home was a local post office and directly outside stood a letter box that would come to see a lot of action.

At the age of 19, Bray wandered into his local post office where a new handbook, published quarterly for post office workers, caught his eye. Despite it not being intended for public reading and containing 500 pages of rather dull regulations, Bray purchased a copy, took it home and read it from cover to cover. Inside, he discovered all sorts of quirks about the postal service: any item could be redirected within 24 hours of delivery; the largest living thing that could be posted was an elephant, the smallest a bee. The trickster in Bray was unleashed. He saw the contents of the handbook as a challenge and from that moment on he would dedicate every waking hour to making mischief with the Royal Mail. Over his lifetime, Bray would come to send over 30,000 singular items through the post.

Not only that – in displaying courage, imagination and ingenuity – Bray would turn postal mischief into an art form. You might even go so far as to describe him as the Picasso of postal art (in fact, we're going to). Not only was he highly original, diverse and ever playful, but just like Picasso with his Rose, Blue and Cubist periods, Bray's work can be divided into distinct stylistic phases.

THE FREAK LETTER PERIOD

Sadly, little remains of Bray's first phase of postal art – a movement he described as 'freak letters' – as most have either rotted away or been lost. Beginning with inanimate objects, Bray posted pretty much anything he could squeeze into the letter box. Items that were too big were marched down to the post office to be weighed and peppered with stamps. Bray posted saucepans, slippers, a half-smoked cigar, seaweed, coins, a rabbit skull, bike pump, clothes brush, cigarettes (with the address written down the side), shirt collars and a turnip (into which

A selection of Bray's curios, including a collar and brush – all successfully delivered through the Royal Mail.

the address was carefully carved). His mother, happy to collude, even crocheted an envelope for him, complete with a minimalist three-word address: BRAY, FOREST HILL. Bray always ensured that a return address was included in his experiments (in case they didn't reach their destination), but his quickly earned notoriety soon meant that those three words would be sufficient for most mail to find its way home to him.

THE LIVING LETTER PERIOD

After mastering the inanimate, Bray turned his attention to the living world. Pre-empting the adventures of Laika, the Soviet space dog sent into orbit by the Russians in 1957, **Bray's Irish terrier Bob** became the first canine to be launched into the Victorians' final frontier, the British postal system. Unlike Laika (who overheated when the thermal insulation in her pod tore loose), Bob lived to tell the tale.

Applying rules found in the 1898 post office handbook stating that, 'a person may be conducted by Express Messenger to any address on payment of mileage charge', Bray's next inevitable experiment was to post himself.

Accompanied by a mail boy, he was safely delivered back to his own home. Bray's stunt made the news and, once again, he reported on the practical value of his prank. He claimed that one night – unable to reach a friend's house owing to the whole of Forest Hill being occluded by a pea souper (a thick poisonous fog) – he took himself to his local post office and was promptly delivered as a letter to his chum's address within minutes. He also suggested that mothers who were too busy to take their children to school could always send them through the mail as parcels.

Three years later he was at it again. This time he sent himself home by registered post, accompanied by his trusty bicycle. One can but wonder how Bray would have reacted to the fact that, 100 years later, an artist would be awarded £10,000 for the same stunt.

LETTERISM

As Bray's art developed, his work began to move from the physical to the cerebral. Turning his attention to the problem-solving skills of the humble postie, he began to

In the first of many newspaper interviews Bray, with typical deadpan humour, declared his experiment in posting Bob to have a practical value: 'Presuming you are sending your dog to a friend or veterinary surgeon and haven't the time yourself, this service will come immediately to your assistance.'

experiment with different ways of presenting an address. First he disguised addresses with backwards handwriting, then he hid them within self-penned poems. After a while, he began to play with pictorial representations – drawing everything from broccoli and ham to wells as pictorial clues, which unravelled like a Holmesian mystery.

While a postcard labelled 'To the proprietor of the most remarkable hotel in the world, somewhere between Santa Cruz and San Jose somehow reached its destination, Bray was not always successful. One postcard, bearing an address written in sealing wax, was promptly returned after most of the writing fell off into his local letter box. Another, penned to 'any Resident of London', was deemed insufficiently addressed, as was a postcard addressed to **Father Christmas Esq**.

As a rule, the Royal Mail responded to Bray's pranks with professional disinterest – delivering the successful ones to their intended destination and returning his failures with the stamp

Bray was one of the first people to write to Santa Claus. It would be another 50 or so years before the postal service began to respond to a growing number of such letters, albeit from slightly younger scribes.

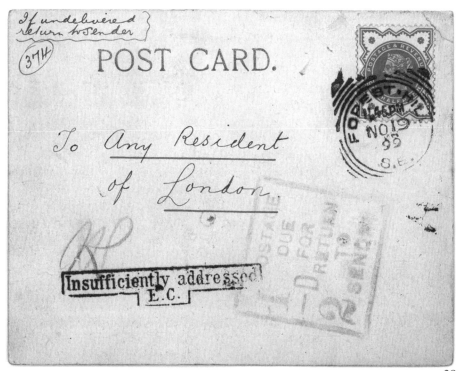

'insufficiently addressed'. Occasionally, however, they would join in the fun. Once, when Bray was required to pay an excess for a letter that had failed to reach its destination, it was returned with the following poem written on the front:

'Pursuing this game
we hope there are not many,
however for your hobby
you'll have to pay a penny.'

With the growing popularity of picture postcards, it was only a matter of time before Bray would find a way to subvert them. He soon hit upon the idea of sending postcards to the person or feature illustrated on the picture side. He addressed a postcard of the Caledonian Express train to its driver, sent a portrait of the Edison Lighthouse to its keeper and mailed postcards of the 'rough sea at Filey' and the Old Man of Hoy (a sea stack in the Orkney archipelago) to their 'nearest residents'. If there were no picture postcards to hand, Bray would simply cut an image out of a magazine, stick that on the cover of a blank postcard, circle it and request for the postcard to be sent there.

THE FAR-OUT PERIOD

For the penultimate phase of Bray's work he turned his attention to geography, with a desire to see not only how far his experiments could travel but by what unconventional means. First, he sealed letters and postcards in bottles and tossed them out to sea. He urged any friends embarking on a sea voyage to take one of his bottles and drop it overboard as far as possible from England. He also persuaded hot-air balloonists to fling his letters out mid-flight attached to smaller balloons. When on trains, Bray would lob stamped mail out of the window attached to *Titbits*, a popular magazine of the time. He reasoned that the finder, delighted in receiving a free copy of the magazine, would be generous enough to post the letter.

One of Bray's most ingenious experiments was to write a letter, address it with the correct postage for its return from, say, Australia and slip it inside a newspaper. He then tied up the newspaper and posted that to a fictional address in Australia.

THE OLD MAN OF HOY, ORKNEY ISLANDS.

After inevitably arriving at a dead letter office in Oz, Bray's newspaper would be unwrapped and the second letter would fall out. Correctly stamped and addressed, it would usually get posted back to England – more often than not to one of Bray's friends.

W. REGINALD BRAY

ALBUMS FOR CHURCHMAN'S PICTURE
CARDS CAN BE OBTAINED FROM
TOBACCONISTS AT ONE PENNY EACH

"IN TOWN TO-NIGHT"

A SERIES OF 50

6

W. REGINALD BRAY
The Human Letter

The owner of the largest collection of postal curios in the British Isles, Mr. Bray was the first man to post himself as a human letter. His collection was started as a hobby in 1898; he made a thorough study of the Post Office Guide and discovered that one of the smallest articles that can be sent by post is a bee, and the largest an elephant! Mr. Bray has posted many peculiar articles, including a shirt front and a collar with the addresses actually written upon them (see illustration). Other things he has sent include a bowler hat, a turnip with the address and message carved on it, a pipe, cigarette, flask, shoes, cycle pump, etc.

W.A. & A.C. CHURCHMAN

ISSUED BY THE IMPERIAL TOBACCO CO.
(OF GREAT BRITAIN & IRELAND), LTD.

Bray's perplexed friends continued to receive his letters from all over the world, while he kept his method secret for over 20 years.

THE AUTOGRAPH KING

Bray wrote to Hitler at least nine times until, finally, Adolf's secretary wrote back politely requesting him to desist as the Führer was far too busy planning to annex the Sudetenland to sign his autograph.

As well as creating postal ephemera, Bray also enjoyed collecting it. Setting himself up as 'The Autograph King', **he collected over 15,000 signatures during his lifetime**. Amassing autographs from famous adventurers, politicians, scientists and war heroes was a popular hobby at the time but Bray, naturally, took it one step further. Reading about a woman who had been kidnapped by Macedonian bandits, he wrote to her requesting her autograph. He then followed this up by tracking down the bandits and requesting theirs, too. He wrote to each of the 208 residents of the remote island of Tristan da Chuna asking for their individual signatures, though was disappointed not to get the full set.

Bray died in 1939 and was immortalized on Churchman's cigarette cards as the first person to post himself through the Royal Mail. As a lover and collector of ephemera, it would have doubtless pleased him to have been remembered this way.

In an age of electronic communication, sending or receiving personal letters is becoming increasingly rare. Mail art is, however, enjoying a resurgence – perhaps as a direct response to the expediency of email, text and social networking. New York artist Ray Johnson is often credited as the godfather of mail art – a movement that developed out of the Fluxus art happenings of the 1950s and '60s. Yet it was Bray, 50 years previously, who should really be championed as the true founder of this movement – a man who dedicated much of his life to bringing creativity, mischief and subversion to a form of mass media that was, in the late 1880s, still in its infancy.

But was Bray really the first human to have been sent through the mail, as he himself believed? Fifty years earlier, in a daring and inventive plan, Henry Brown escaped slavery in Richmond, Virginia, by mailing himself to the free state of Pennsylvania. He spent much of his 24-hour journey upside down in a box marked 'special delivery of dry goods', travelling by train and steamer before emerging, bruised and battered, 300 miles from his old home, a free man. Originality in art remains a rare and precious thing. DB

KEN CAMPBELL

The seeker who sought to astound

Ken Campbell: the name may not be familiar but what about the bald pate, impish grin and eyebrows like an abandoned allotment? Perhaps you saw him in 'The Anniversary' episode of *Fawlty Towers*, playing the irritating Roger, or as the solicitor Bartlett in *A Fish Called Wanda*?

Campbell was a performer, comic, theatre director and creative powerhouse but the reason for his inclusion in this book lies in a Facebook group called 'Ken Campbell Changed My life'. Along with an impressive list of actors and comics who worked under Campbell's zealous tutorage the group numbers thousands of fellow 'seekers' – those inspired by Campbell's mind, his storytelling and sense of mischief. For Campbell, the whole of life was one 'great caper', a mission to seek out 'the other'. What was the other? Anything that had the power to astound. And Campbell was a rare individual who possessed such power.

> 'There is a meaning to life that can be peripherally sensed by being astounded or astounding others. And it may be fully glimpsed by astounding yourself.'
> –*Ken Campbell's Meaning of Life* (2006)

Campbell first came into prominence in the late 1960s with an anarchic comedy ensemble, *The Ken Campbell Roadshow*, which included **Sylvester McCoy**, Bob Hoskins and dwarf actor, David Rappaport – who Ken would introduce as 'not the world's smallest man, but fucking close!' His ensemble mixed comedy with music-hall stunts – nails up the nose, ferrets down the trousers – with McCoy always as the fall guy. Side-stepping theatre's elitism, dwindling audiences and funding bodies, Ken took his roadshow into working men's clubs and pubs, often unannounced. 'If the

Years later, when the BBC were deliberating on whether to choose Campbell or McCoy as the seventh Dr Who, it was McCoy who won out; Campbell being deemed too much of a wild card.

audience won't come to us, we'll go to them,' became their motto.

Almost from the start, Campbell's theatre work was anarchic and unconventional. Inspired by childhood sci-fi books with titles like *Astounding Stories* and *Amazing Tales*, in 1976 he co-founded the Science Fiction Theatre of Liverpool. Applying the principle, 'If you want people to work for nothing, you're better off doing something impossible', the first production, *Illuminatus!,* ran for over eight hours. It was based on Robert Anton Wilson and Robert Shea's complex cult sci-fi trilogy and it had a huge cast including Bill Nighy and Jim Broadbent, with miniature sets designed by Bill Drummond (later to be half of The KLF). The science fiction author Brian Aldiss said the show 'made Wagner's Ring Cycle seem like a frog's arsehole'.

Ken was also the winner of the 'most number of sink plungers stuck on on a human head' award, an honour he dreamed up and to which he was the only contestant. The winning number was five, as demonstrated live in his one-man show, 'Jamais Vu'.

After this, the only option was to up the ante. In 1979, Campbell entered the **Guinness Book of Records** by co-writing and directing the world's longest play. *The Warp* was an autobiographical tale of one man's journey of self-discovery through beat culture, jazz, scientology, New Age and psychedelia. It ends at a flying saucer conference in 1968.

The Warp boasted a cast of 50 with live musicians and plenty of pharmaceutical assistance. Russell Denton, who remained on stage for nearly all 22 hours, managed to impress Campbell (no mean feat) by learning the entire script in three weeks. That's the equivalent to six *Hamlet*s. Those who saw *The Warp* or starred in it were never the same again.

THE ROYAL DICKENS SOCIETY

In 1980, Campbell pulled off one of the greatest pranks in British history. The Royal Shakespeare Company (RSC), then headed by Trevor Nunn, had recently staged an eight-hour version of *Nicholas Nickleby* at the Aldridge Theatre in London, which had been well received. Put out that in creating an epic theatre show they were treading on his turf, Campbell procured a letter with the RSC logo and Trevor Nunn's signature.

He then approached his friends at the Anarchist Press and persuaded them to modify the letterhead so that it read RDC: the Royal Dickens Theatre. He went on to individually write to hundreds of people in the theatre world – including the Arts Council and Minister for the Arts – to inform them of a 'major policy change'. In his letters, he sketched out a potential cast for the RDC's next production of *Little Dorrit,* inviting actors, directors and producers to get involved.

The hoax caused much embarrassment in the theatre world. Trevor Nunn was quoted in the press as saying: 'a lot of people have written refusing or, more embarrassingly, accepting'. It didn't help when posters with the RDC logo and an advert for the forthcoming production of *Little Dorrit* began to appear round London. It wasn't until Nunn called in Scotland Yard that Campbell finally owned up on BBC2's *Newsnight,* claiming to presenter Jeremy Paxman that he'd only done it 'to highlight what a terrific job the RSC do'.

Truth was, Campbell was cocking a snoop at one of the UK's great institutions; it was a wanton act of rebellion against heavily funded 'high art'. It was also just another part of 'the great caper', done to amuse (or astound) himself as much as those around him.

As was his decision to establish an 'office' in the centre of London's Hackney Marshes in the 1980s. Decked out in a fisherman's jacket (with specially constructed miniature drawers for pockets), Campbell would sit at his desk in the middle of a field for days on end, doing 'marsh business'. On hot summer afternoons, **his eyebrows** – which took on a life of their own in later years – were pinned back out of his eyes with clothes pegs.

SEEKER OF THE NEXT GREAT CAPER

Campbell touched the lives of thousands, but was far from easy to work with. He could chastise and bully his actors and was never afraid to throw his opinion around at the top of his voice. As one performer put it: 'Ken came out of the womb absolutely certain about everything.' Friends often found themselves being performed at rather than spoken to. But Campbell's mischief and enthusiasm were so infectious, who wouldn't want to be swept up in the next great caper?

During the late 1990s, Campbell dated performer Nina Conti and persuaded her to take up the (deeply unfashionable) art of ventriloquism. Conti found she had a knack for it, but doubted she would ever make it as a performer. After Campbell's death, however, she discovered he had bequeathed her his collection of

While Campbell's eyebrows became increasingly unruly over the years, they couldn't be trimmed – they were too valuable an asset in getting him acting jobs playing the mad professor.

As an aside, Campbell was rather fond of books filled with footnotes.

He was especially fond of footnotes of footnotes.

Royal Dickens Theatre

Stratford-upon-Avon Warwickshire CV37 6BB
Telephone: (0789) 296655
Box Office Telephone: (0789) 292271

14th July, 1980

Dear Lindsay,

As you have probably heard, there has been a major policy change in our organisation.

"Nicholas Nickleby" has been such a source of real joy to cast, staff and audience that we have decided to turn to Dickens as our main source of inspiration.

So that'll be it for the bard as soon as our present commitments decently permit.

The first production of the new RDC is hoped to be "Little Dorrit", adapted by Snoo Wilson, and directed by John Caird and myself.

Thinking of you, Lindsay, brings the Old Curiosity Shop to mind. What a coup if you could bring Sir Ralph and Sir John together again in a script by David Storey for this venture. I feel your cool, intelligent approach is going to be badly needed here in these new times.

I look forward to hearing your reactions.

Love,

Trev

also in Stratford-upon-Avon at The Other Place and in London at the Aldwych Theatre and The Warehouse.

Royal Dickens Company
JOINT ARTISTIC DIRECTORS Terry Hands Trevor Nunn
DIRECTION Peggy Ashcroft John Barton Peter Brook Terry Hands Trevor Nunn

Royal Dickens Theatre Incorporated under Royal Charter PATRON Her Majesty the Queen
PRESIDENT Sir Harold Wilson CHAIRMAN Sir Kenneth Cork VICE CHAIRMAN Dennis L Flower

who kept his

ventriloquist dolls and insisted she go to the World Ventriloquist Convention in Kentucky to lay one of his dolls to rest in its graveyard, Vent Haven. From beyond the grave, Campbell created a caper for Conti, who made a BBC documentary of her adventures in *Her Master's Voice* and became the UKs best-loved TV ventriloquist - if not, the only one.

Throughout the 1990s, Campbell toured a string of one-man shows that plundered his life stories and adventures. A fantastical blend of fact and fiction, they were, for the most part, delivered on stage with nothing more than the odd prop. Subject matter veered wildly from Cathar heretics and Jackie Chan to Stephen Hawking's idea of the multiverse and teleportation. One show, *Hyphenator*, began with the lines:

> 'At the age of 64 I was sent out by **my daughter** with £600 and strict instructions to buy a computer. But on the way I passed a pet shop and found that, for a few pounds more, I could upgrade and buy a parrot.'

It was a classic caper, an autobiographical Jack and the Beanstalk tale in which Ken discovers his parrot Doris has a flair for art, leading him to arrange great exhibitions of her 'pecktures' (a combination of bird poo and coloured paper she'd nibbled away at). In another show, *Pigspurt*, Campbell recounts how his nose had grown to resemble the back and thighs of a naked woman, leading him on a Cinderella-esque search to find this elusive female. In *Jamais Vu*, Ken tells of his travels to Vanuatu in the South Pacific to meet the tribes on the island of Tanna who **worship Prince Philip** as a god.

The customs of the South Pacific were to be a recurring theme in Campbell's work, leading him to champion Bislama – the strand of Pidgin English spoken on Tanna – as an obvious choice for a *wal wantok* (world language). Bislama consists of little more than 400 words – *handbag* being the rudest – and with minimal grammar: 'Subjunctives they looked into, but reckoned they'd not really brought anyone any happiness.'

Forget Esperanto, Ken argued, Bislama can be learned in a few hours. Owing to its paucity of words, to Campbell, speaking Bislama merely required a creative imagination. 'We could have

In 2014 Ken Campbell's daughter Daisy Campbell staged an epic theatre production of Robert Anton Wilson's *Comsic Trigger* in Liverpool and London. Both Daisy and her dad feature as characters in the play, along with Timothy Leary and Alan Watts.

Campbell loved to re-tell the story (which he discovered in Tim Heald's book *The Duke*), that if the Queen were ever to accompany her husband to Tanna and witness him drinking the local brew, kava, she would be instantly executed by a single blow to the head with a kava root.

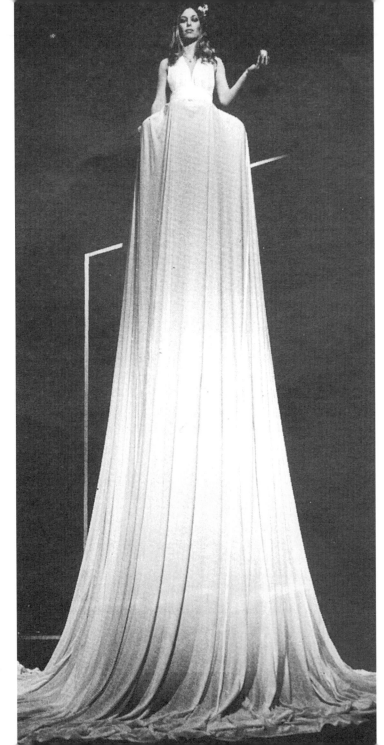

Prunella Gee as Eris,
the goddess of
discord and chaos in
Ken's adaptation of
The Illuminatus! Trilogy
(1975)

a world language by Thursday if I was in charge,' he proclaimed.

However, it would probably take until Thursday to tell anyone about it. With such a dearth of words, **simple English phrases could be stretched out to ridiculously lengths**. The word for Prince Philip is *Nambawan bigfala emi blong Misis Kwin*.

Gearing up for another caper, with the help of some drama students Ken translated *Macbeth* into Pidgin and, using only didgeridoos as props, took *Makbed blong Willum Sekspia* on tour. Halfway through the play, when Lady Macbeth is offering her soul to the devil in exchange for her husband taking the crown, the lines 'Come you spirits that tend on mortal thoughts, unsex me here' translated into Pidgin as: 'Satan, come take me handbag.'

In his autumn years, Campbell moved into a giant shed in Epping Forest with his parrot Doris and two dogs. He would tell audiences about how he was plagued with what he called the 'bathroom shelf issue'. Those who visited would notice the shelf – with Ken's shaving and teeth-cleaning accoutrements – lying on the floor by the sink. Ken would explain: 'I ought to put it up; the only problem is, there's always something far more interesting to be done instead.' He died suddenly in 2008 at the age of 66, the caper complete; the shelf still lying on the bathroom floor. DB

In Pidgin, piano translates as: *wan bigfala blak bokis hemi gat waet tut mo hemi gat blak tut, sipos yu kilim smol, hemi singaot gud*. Literally: 'one big fella black box, him he got white tooth and (or more/in addition to) him he got black tooth, suppose you kill him small (strike or hit lightly) him he sing out good.'

SEVEN STEPS TO TURNING YOUR OWN LIFE INTO A CAMPBELLIAN CAPER*

1 Ask yourself, is it heroic?
2 Remember that funded means 'fun dead'.
3 Believing is mind-deadening; supposing is mind-expanding.
4 If you want people to work for nothing, you're better off attempting something impossible.
5 Read science fiction. When you think about it, the whole history of literature is just people going in and out of doors; science fiction is about everything else.
6 If it's not as interesting as a man with a firework up his arse, then it's lacking quotient X.
7 There is no Self. But it might just be possible to astound a Self into being.

*As suggested by members of the 'Ken Campbell Changed My Life' Facebook group

PRINCE ROY OF SEALAND

The buccaneer who founded a micronation

In 1949, Ealing Studios released what would become one of their best-loved comedies, *Passport to Pimlico*. Set in London during the Second World War, the film begins with the discovery of an ancient parchment in an underground chamber. The document reveals that Pimlico was once ceded by Edward IV to the last Duke of Burgundy. As the charter was never revoked Pimlico is still, officially, part of the country of Burgundy. Pimlico's residents, on hearing this and realizing they are no longer legally bound to the laws of England, declare themselves to be an independent state. The authorities respond by putting barbed wire around their newly-formed principality and 'closing the border'. Chaos ensues.

Curiously, part of the inspiration for the script was a real-life incident during the Second World War when a maternity ward in Ottawa was declared by the Canadian government to be an independent state. With Holland's exiled queen about to give birth to Princess Margriet of the Netherlands, it was the only way to avoid her daughter losing her right to the throne.

RISE OF THE MICRONATIONS

While both of these would appear to be rather unusual tales, since the 1940s the world has seen a steady increase in tiny, independent sovereign states. Unrecognized by world governments, these micronations are sometimes a symbol of defiance by political activists (trying to protect a building or sacred space) or, more commonly, the work of mischief-makers who fancy donning regal garb and bossing everyone about. This is certainly the case with the Kingdom of Elleore in Denmark, set up as a bit of fun on the island of Elleore in 1944 by a group of schoolteachers, and France's Republic of Saugeais, established in 1947 by the self-titled President Georges Pourchet. America,

Molossia has even
appointed its own
Ministry for Air and
Space Exploration,
responsible for the
micronation's small
rocket fleet. Launches
include *Astrocam*
(crashed, too 'nose
heavy'), *Hypérion*
(40 balloons tied to a
camera, which flew to
23 feet, or 7 meters,
then landed in a tree),
the *Endeavour*
(launched successfully,
although the video
turned out not to be
compatible with
Windows Vista) and
Marilyn (Molossia's
first attempt at getting
live creatures aloft;
four Mexican jumping
beans returned to the
ground safely and the
mission was declared
a success!).

unsurprisingly, is full of them – including the **Republic of Molossia in Nevada**, Conch Republic in Key West and the Kingdom of Calsahara in California (current population: three).

There is one micronation, however, which has done more than any other to establish itself legitimately as a new independent principality. Sealand is often labelled the 'textbook micronation'. It is also one of the most curious and piratical tales to have emerged in recent English history.

During the Second World War, the British military built a number of sea forts in international waters along the east coast as part of the UK's defence against a possible invasion from Germany. Among these were the Maunsell Naval Sea Forts, six miles off the Suffolk coast. These artificial islands, measuring almost 6,000 square feet (550 square metres) each, were once home to hundreds of naval personnel until they were abandoned in 1956. For a short while they remained four silent metal ghost villages just visible to the naked eye from the ports of Harwich and Ispwich.

By the mid-1960s, the explosion in pop music and counter-culture in the UK had seen a rising demand for pop music on the radio. The BBC however, had exclusive rights to the airwaves and lacked, as one critic put it, 'decent music or palatable presenters'. In respond to public demand, and in what could best be described as an early form of hacking, a band of radio pirates squatted the UK's abandoned sea forts and started broadcasting round-the-clock pop music.

The most notorious pirate radio DJ was Screaming Lord Sutch, who would go on to greater fame by forming the Monster Raving Loony Party. The party's main policies were the protection of unicorns and the abolishment of income tax, arguing that it was 'only meant to be a temporary measure, having been set up to pay for the Napoleonic War'. The party proved to be popular. By the mid-1990s, it had 16 councillors and sponsorship from Monster Munch. But we digress.

These buccaneers of the airwaves soon became piratical in the traditional sense. Rivalry between stations led to clashes, violence and, in one instance, a broadcaster being killed over an argument about a transmitter. Of the four Maunsell sea forts, Rough Towers was the only one occupied by a pirate radio station. After a skirmish, however, its occupiers were forcibly

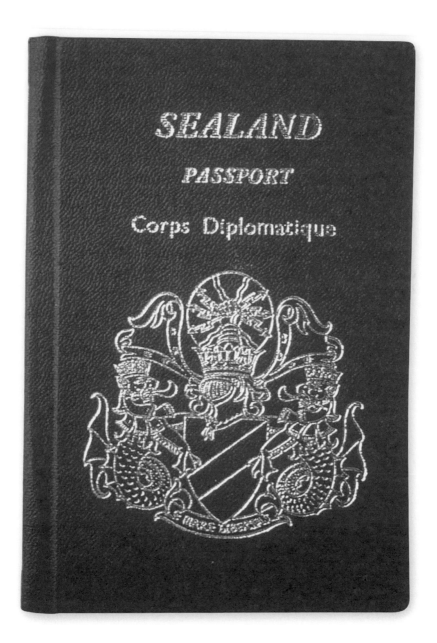

evicted by a competing pirate radio station led by Roy Bates, his family and several armed friends. Bates continued to defend the fort with guns and petrol bombs, despite an order to surrender by the British authorities. On 2 September 1967, Bates declared himself Prince Roy of Sealand; his wife became Princess Joan. It was her birthday and she told Roy it was the best present she'd ever had.

After a court case eventually ruled that, as Bates was outside England's legally controlled area, he was free to do what he wanted. The government, worried by the implications, immediately destroyed the remaining Maunsell towers for fear of other micronations springing up.

By 1975, Sealand had a flag, a national anthem, postage stamps, currency and passports. Anyone who entered its exclusion zone uninvited was shot at. At any one time a dozen or so people lived on Sealand and, while life aboard couldn't have been particularly comfortable, they were only ever a short helicopter or boat ride back to the mainland.

Three years later, in 1978, Prince Roy was lured away from his micronation to Austria for a meeting with Alexander Achenbach, a German businessman who claimed to be interested in turning Sealand into a casino. It was a scam. With Roy safely off Sealand, Achenbach landed by helicopter with his lawyer and associates, locked up Roy's son Michael for three days without provisions, then effectively made him walk the plank by putting him out to sea on a boat.

When Roy got wind of what had happened he returned with armed assistants, evicted the intruders, picked up his son and kept Achenbach's lawyer as hostage. He then threw the book at the lawyer, sentenced him for treason and gave him 'life' in Sealand's jail. After six weeks, Germany, recognizing a diplomatic crisis, sent a diplomat to secure his release. Had Sealand chosen to execute the lawyer, they would have been answerable to no laws other than their own.

So why was Sealand so desirable? Roy Bates cleverly turned the accident of statehood into his core business. Sealand has to date issued 150,000 passports. They offer aristocratic titles such as Lord, Lady or Baroness of Sealand for a very reasonable £30 and, since the turn of the millennium, have leased their country to HavenCo Limited, which offers 'unparalleled security

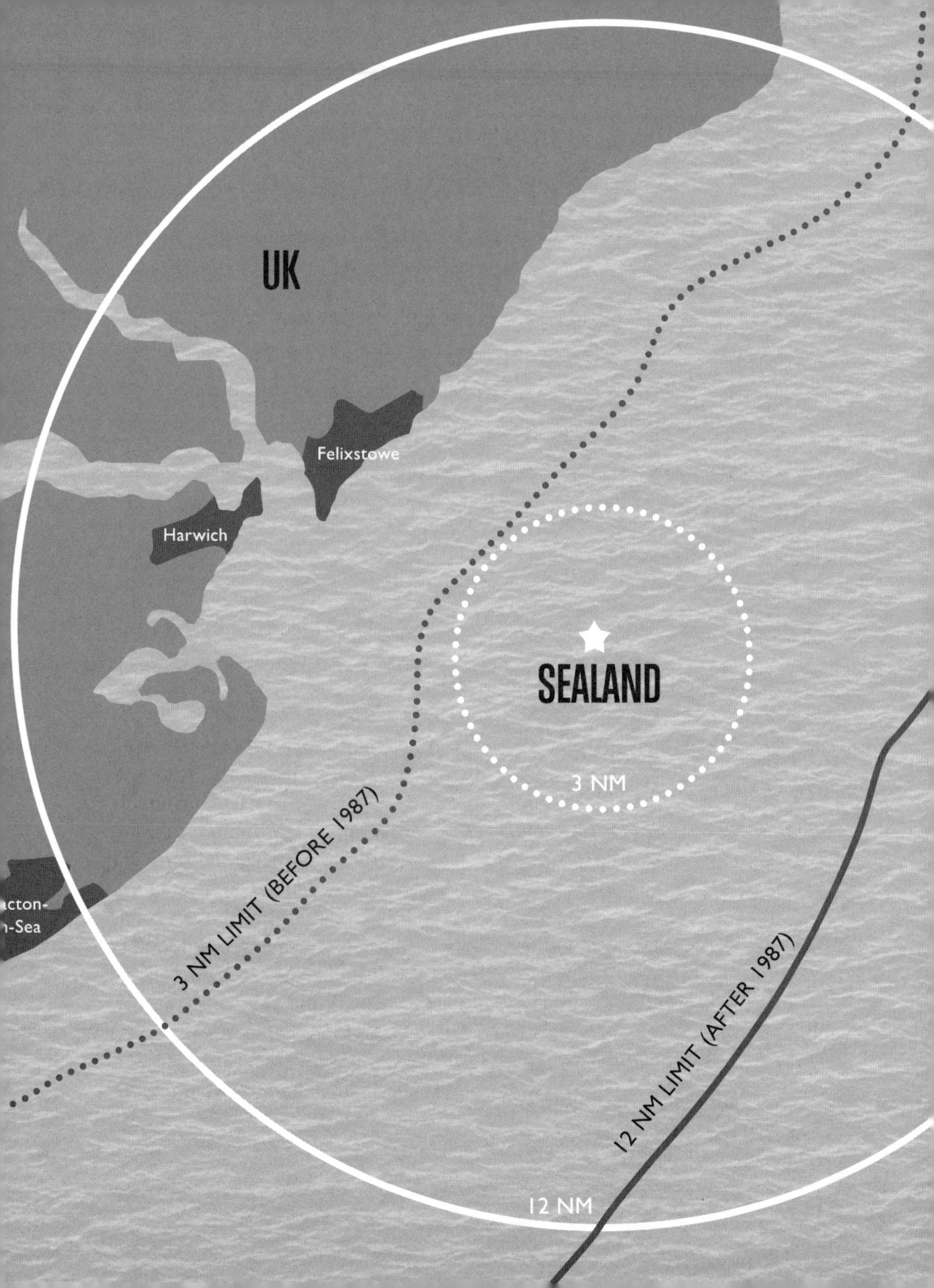

UK

Felixstowe

Harwich

SEALAND

3 NM

3 NM LIMIT (BEFORE 1987)

cton-
-Sea

12 NM LIMIT (AFTER 1987)

12 NM

and independence to users who wish to take advantage of its Internet services'. Sealand continues to attract the interests of those seeking sanctuary from the law, including WikiLeaks, who considered moving its servers to the principality and, appropriately, Pirate Bay, the 'galaxy's most resilient BitTorrent site'.

In 1987, in accordance with changes in international laws, Britain extended its territorial waters from 3 to 12 nautical miles, which meant that Sealand could be claimed as being in British waters. In response, Sealand extended its own territorial waters by the same distance, claiming that, if Britain now owned Sealand, Sealand, in turn, now owned the towns of Felixstowe and Harwich and the nicer parts of Clacton-on-Sea.

Sealand's original royalty no longer reside at Sealand. Roy Bates retired to the mainland and died in 2012. His son and heir is now Prince of Sealand. Nowadays the micronation's population rarely exceeds five.

Despite still not being officially recognized as an independent principality, no attempts have ever been made by UK authorities to claim Sealand back. It remains an anomaly in the North Sea – a tenacious band of pirates. Should you fancy visiting, it's best not to turn up unannounced. Shots are still fired at vessels that enter Sealand's extended exclusion zone. And if you have been lucky enough to be invited, don't forget your passport. *DB*

1:08

MAGGIE AND KATE FOX

The teens who awoke the spirit world

During the mid-1800s, a new movement began to sweep across America and Europe. In households and city venues, windows were blacked out, hands held, spirits evoked, tables levitated and ectoplasm coughed up until – finally – the disembodied spirit of someone's Uncle Peter manifested from beyond the grave to inform his nearest and dearest that all was well in the afterlife and could they please remember to feed his cat.

At the height of its popularity, spiritualism had millions of devoted followers who believed in the afterlife, together with an array of celebrity clairvoyants and mediums to open the door between the worlds of spirit and matter. Those who didn't have 'the gift' could take advantage of special mail-order catalogues that openly sold fake hands, bottled ectoplasm and chair-rattling devices. Sceptics were drowned in a sea of believers. But how did it all start? As all fans of horror movies will know, whenever there's spectral activity, a sensitive teenage girl is never far away. When there's two of them under one roof, however, that's when things can really get out of hand.

On 11 December 1847, John and Margaret Fox, together with their two youngest daughters, moved into an old farmhouse in Hydesville, outside of New York. The building had a reputation for being haunted and, sure enough, within a few weeks the couple began to hear mysterious noises. Margaret, susceptible to matters of the spirit world, took it to be evidence of a ghost. The strange sounds continued for several weeks, as if someone was creeping around the house. Had Margaret burst in on her daughters during these witching hours she would have discovered the guilty pair holding an apple on a piece of string and rhythmically banging it on to the floor.

Seeing as the girls were of a butter-wouldn't-melt deposition, however, such an idea never crossed Margaret's mind. Having successfully spooked their poor mother, Maggie and Kate took the lark one step further. In learning how to snap their fingers and toes, the pair began to claim they could communicate with the spirit. Maggie snapped her fingers and the spirit (in the guise of Maggie's or Kate's big toe) responded with a click of its own. Before long the girls were asking it questions using the classic one click for 'yes', two for 'no' and three for 'whoooo'.

Questioning of the spirit became more sophisticated when the family began to substitute numbers for letters of the alphabet. The spirit revealed its name to be Mr Splitfoot – an old moniker for the devil – who later transformed into Charles Rosma, a peddler who claimed to have been murdered in the house five years before the Foxes settled in. After neighbours witnessed the spirit rapping and swore it to be genuine, word spread through the community. The prank took a more sinister turn, however, when previous occupants of the house were tracked down and investigated by various neighbours. The general consensus was that the murder had been committed by a former tenant named Bell. While his guilt couldn't be proven, Bell was ostracized from the community.

SPILLING THE BEANS

Kate and Maggie, having now gone too far into the woods to return, moved to Rochester to live with their older sister, Leah, a single mum of 33. After wrestling the secret out of her younger siblings, Leah saw dollar signs and set to work organizing séances, over which she would preside. It wasn't long before the trio were besieged with requests up and down the country.

Maggie and Kate, managed by Leah, became established mediums, conducting large-scale séances that paid handsomely. Other folk claiming to have psychic powers soon began to step forward. The vast majority of mediums were young women or pubescent girls whose souls, it was believed, were still pure enough for the spirits to be channelled through.

Many came forward to challenge spiritualism, including Harry Houdini who made it his primary mission later in life to expose **'phony mediums'**. Despite his success, vast numbers of believers could not be swayed. Across America and Europe, mortality

Houdini was interested in spiritualism as he wanted to contact his mother, but he only met with frauds. To prove he was open-minded, however, he made a pact with his friends that when he died he would attempt to make contact with them. He even devised a secret code that only his wife, Bess, could decipher. Following his death in 1926, a man named Arthur Ford delivered a message that Bess validated. The case remains open.

rates were high; one in three children died in childbirth and war had claimed the lives of thousands. Every family was touched by death; spiritualism offered solace.

Over time, Leah split from her siblings and moved to New York, where she set herself up as a medium. Her sisters continued to tour until 1852, when Maggie married explorer Elisha Kent Kane, 13 years her senior and sceptical of her spirit powers. Although unable to figure out how his wife did the tapping, he begged her to give up her 'dreary life'. Maggie conceded and converted to Catholicism, but after her husband's untimely death a few years later she began to drink heavily and returned to clairvoyance.

On 21 October 1888, Maggie (having fallen out with Leah) decided to spill the beans at a planned public appearance at the New York Academy of Music. Kate was in the audience for moral support; both now had serious drink problems and were feeling deep remorse for their years of deception. Before a large audience, Maggie revealed her simple means of creating a disembodied rapping sound by snapping her big toe. Before leaving the stage she thanked God she was finally able to expose spiritualism as a sham. The movement carried on as if nothing had happened.

Several years later, Maggie recanted her words, doubtless out of poverty. However, by now the Fox sisters had all been discredited in the eyes of both the public and the spiritualist movement they founded. Both died of drink-related illnesses a few years later.

While losing momentum after the First World War, spiritualism remains an active force in the world. Like the *Sorcerer's Apprentice*, the sisters unleashed a monster they couldn't put back in the box; one which, ultimately, led to their early demise.

Although spiritualism was built on deceit, it also gave unprecedented opportunities for women to speak their minds and promote popular causes of temperance and abolishment of slavery. As a movement, it put equality at its centre of its doctrine. Maggie and Kate had, unwittingly, set the ball rolling for suffragettes, black rights and the liberal values of the 20th century. Quite a legacy for a pair of teenagers who set out just to spook their mum. DB

1:09

SCREAMING LORD SUTCH

The politician who lost 40 elections

It's the 1998 Brit Awards and anarcho-punk band Chumbawamba have just performed their hit single, 'Tubthumping'. Later that evening, band member Danbert Nobacon spies Labour politician John Prescott in the audience. Annoyed at Prescott's refusal to support a recent dockers' strike, Nobacon alights a chair and proceeds to pour a bucket of ice water over the politician's head, announcing, 'This is for the Liverpool dockers', before beating a hasty retreat (Prescott is not shy of using his fists). Nobacon's stunt makes the British headlines but divides opinion among his peers. Jarvis Cocker, who had invaded the Brit Awards stage two years earlier to wiggle his bum at Michael Jackson, expresses disdain. Malcolm McLaren, former manager of the Sex Pistols, applauds it.

Nobacon's act of dissent may have been misplaced, perhaps even cowardly, but how often do any of us get close enough to politicians to really let them know how we feel? There was once a time when a fool – typified in *King Lear* – was present in court to challenge those in power with his wit and 'bullshit detector'. Nowadays, our politicians are surrounded by a ring of armed henchmen; satirists are restricted to social media and comedy stores. There is, however, one sure-fire way to rub shoulders with politicians – a chance to poke, prod and ridicule them face to face – and that is to form your own political party.

Uniquely (in British culture at least), this is precisely what one man did for 30 years, embarking on a lifelong campaign to bring humour and colour to the political arena – and, in the process, put more than a few political noses out of joint.

It may be a cliché, but David Sutch really was a quintessential English eccentric. A working-class lad with a taste for theatrics, he began performing in his teens. By the early 1960s, he had a minor hit with the song 'Jack the Ripper'. Inspired by 1950s horror movies and musician Screaming Jay Hawkins, Sutch adopted the name Screaming Lord Sutch and would emerge on stage from a coffin, sporting long black hair, theatrical make-up and trademark leopardskin coat and top hat, to sing a ghoulish repertoire that included 'Dracula's Daughter', 'All Black and Hairy' and 'Monster Rock'. He also dabbled in pirate radio by launching Radio Sutch from Shivering Sands, one of the Maunsell Sea Forts, until his manager Reg Calvert was shot dead by a rival pirate radio producer.

Desiring to shake up the staid and colourless world of British politics, in 1963 Sutch formed the National Teenage Party, advocating the right for 18-year-olds to vote (the voting age, at the time, was 21). While largely intended as a satirical comment on politicians acting like teenagers, it fuelled debate and six years later the law changed in his favour.

Sutch also experimented with the Go to Blazes Party and Sod 'Em All Party but, after hearing himself described as a 'raving lunatic' by a Tory candidate, he found inspiration for his final political party, whose new slogan would be: 'Vote for insanity, you know it makes sense.'

THE PEOPLE VERSUS MAGGIE

The Monster Raving Loony Party formed in 1982. The following year, Sutch stood against Margaret Thatcher in a by-election. He could often be seen cradling a giant tin-opener to 'open up the Iron Lady'. While causing great mirth for many, he failed to get sufficient votes and lost his deposit. Having clearly got up Thatcher's nose, the following year she increased the deposit required to stand for election from £150 to £500.

Over the next 16 years, Sutch led and lost 40 by-elections (and a great deal of money), always holding his 'victory party' the evening before the general election to 'avoid disappointment'. Throughout the 1980s and 1990s, when elections were pending, Sutch would pop up on the TV and in the papers, dressed as always in his top hat and leopardskin coat blazoned with badges and slogans. By now, any serious policies he had once proffered (and often seen come to fruition) such as 24-hour licences for pubs and passports for pets had been replaced with silly ones. The official party policies now included: the abolition of income tax, the protection of unicorns and the introduction of a 99p coin. The party's manifesto also noted that, in the event of any member being elected, he/she would be immediately expelled from the party.

At the height of its notoriety, the Monster Raving Loony Party had 16 local councillors, sponsorship from Monster Munch and had found its way into the *Guinness Book of Records* for losing the most number of parliamentary elections in UK history. Occasionally, their antics even impacted on established political parties. After Lord Sutch won more votes than the Social Democratic Party (SDP) at a 1990 by-election, the SDP's humiliated leader, David Owen, had no choice but resign.

As a musician, Sutch never ranked higher than a one-hit wonder. He recorded a handful of albums and, despite persuading such rock gods as Keith Moon, Jimmy Page, John Bonham and Jeff Beck to play with him, his LP *Lord Sutch and Heavy Friends* was voted the 'worst album ever made' in a 1998 BBC poll. As a political subversive, however, he was the Elvis of his day. A gaudily dressed and unwelcome gatecrasher, he brought humour and colour to the tired and lumbering British political system – one that remains dominated by a privileged but drab elite.

Like many extroverts, Sutch's private persona was rather different from his public facade. He suffered mood swings and depression throughout his life; he struggled to hold down relationships and lived with his mother for most of his life. He took her death in 1997 badly and, two years later, hung himself with a skipping rope. It was a sad end for a man who, to the outside world at least, didn't take life too seriously.

Despite his tragic passing, the Monster Raving Loony Party lives on – headed by candidates with names such as Howling Laud Hope and Mad Max Bobestsky. It remains a playground for the kind of people who like to ride penny farthings, wear loud blazers, quote Monty Python sketches and drink real ale. They **continue to mix practical policies with the inane**: their latest manifesto proclaims that in future all socks should be sold in packs of three, to safeguard against losing one. *DB*

Their policies fit neatly in a handy A–Z: A is for AIR bags fitted to the Stock Exchange, ready for the next crash; H is for HALF the grey squirrels to be painted red to increase the red squirrel population; Q is for QUITTERS, encouraged not to start in the first place to improve their self-esteem; Z is for ZEBRA crossings, which will be made available to all animals wishing to cross the road.

SEEKERS' DIRECTORY

TUESDAY LOBSANG RAMPA

BOOK Hoskin wrote 20 books under the name Lobsang Rampa, which you can pick up for peanuts in charity shops. Look out for *The Third Eye* (1956), *Living with the Lama* (1964), *As It Was!* (1976).

RADIO PLAY *The Third Eye and the Private Eye* (2015), BBC Radio 4

ALBUM Peace and tranquillity, delivered in a strong West Country accent; Dr T. Lobsang Rampa, *Meditation* (1969)

HARRY BENSLEY

ARCHIVE *Man in the Iron Mask* is an online resource compiled by Bensley's descendants
mcnaught.orpheusweb.co.uk/HarryB

JOE ORTON

FIELD TRIP See Orton and Halliwell's handiwork at Islington Local History Centre, London N5 1PF

FILM *Prick Up Your Ears* (1987), a superb film with Gary Oldman as Orton, Alfred Molina as Halliwell and screenplay by Alan Bennett

BOOK *The Orton Diaries* (1986), edited by John Lahr

BOOK Ilsa Colsell, *Malicious Damage: The Defaced Library Books of Kenneth Halliwell and Joe Orton* (2013).

EMPEROR NORTON

BIOGRAPHY William Drury, *Norton I, Emperor of the United States* (1986)

WALKING TOUR Emperor Norton's Fantastic San Francisco Time Machine,
emperornortontour.com

W REGINALD BRAY

BOOK John Tingey, *The Englishman Who Posted Himself and Other*

Curious Objects (2010) – this thoughtfully designed book gives a thorough insight into the life of the great postal prankster.

ARCHIVE W. Reginald Bray,
wrbray.org.uk

KEN CAMPBELL

BIOGRAPHY Jeff Merrifield, *Seeker!: Ken Campbell: Five Amazing Lives* (2001)

AUDIO *Wol Wantok* (2000) – Ken Campbell's hilarious rendition of *Macbeth* in pidgin English

MONOLOGUES Few quality recordings remain of Campbell's work, beyond a hotch-potch of teasers and clips on YouTube and a few audio recordings of solo shows. Transcripts of four of his one-man shows are available in book form but are best read once you've become familiar with Campbell's excitable, nasal twang. *The Bald Trilogy:* 'Recollections of a Furtive Nudist', 'Pigspurt', 'Jamais Vu' (1995)

FACEBOOK PAGE 'Ken Campbell Changed My Life'

DOCUMENTARY *Her Master's Voice* (2012), presented by Nina Conti

PODCAST *Odditorium Episode 10: The Cosmic Trigger Play with Daisy Campbell*, oddpodcast.com

ROY BATES

TITLE Become a lord, lady, baron or baroness of Sealand –
sealandgov.org/shop

RADIO DOCUMENTARY *In Living Memory*, series 16, episode 1, BBC Radio 4

FIELD TRIP Visit Felixstowe with a pair of binoculars.

KATE AND MAGGIE FOX

BOOK David Chapin, *Exploring Other Worlds* (2004)

SCREAMING LORD SUTCH

POLITICAL PARTY Join the party to receive your rosette, certificate of insanity and official Loony Party ID card - loonyparty.com

SINGLE Lord's Sutch's LP *Lord Sutch and Heavy Friends* (1970), featuring Keith Moon, Jimmy Page, John Bonham and Jeff Beck, was voted the 'worst album ever made' in a 1998 BBC poll. However, it's worth looking up 1964 recordings of Sutch performing 'Jack the Ripper' to a host of screaming young fans.

2

CREATIVE MAVERICKS

2

CREATIVE MAVERICKS

During his decades as a college lecturer, author Joseph Campbell was often asked the same question by his students: 'Mr Campbell, do you think I could be an artist?' His reply was always the same: 'Of course I do. But do you think you could endure a potential lifetime of poverty, obscurity and disappointment? If you do, then you have it in you to be an artist.'

Campbell was not mincing words. The difficult and painful lives of Van Gogh, Poe and Kafka are, to all struggling artists, a stark reminder that posthumous applause is cold comfort. For those driven by a creative streak, a keen eye on the Zeitgeist and commercial market offers the best chance of survival. To the outsider artist, however, there appears no choice but to do it their way or not at all, whatever the consequences. It is these artists – though often shocking, bizarre or incomprehensible in their lifetimes – who become the pioneers of new art forms and movements, previously unimaginable.

SATURN

NEPTUN

URANUS

This chapter offers a disparate selection of uncompromising, stubborn and heroic individuals, many of whom risked their status, security and sanity to pursue their singular visions. Some, like poet Edith Sitwell and artist Baroness Elsa von Freytag-Loringhoven, were so ahead of their game that they were largely ignored or mocked during their lifetimes. The Baroness Elsa, we will discover, may well deserve credit for what many consider the single most important work of art in the 20th century, Marcel Duchamp's *Fountain*.

Others endured a lifetime of hardship to win the appreciation they deserved. For the blind musician Moondog, it took 30 years busking the streets of New York dressed as a Viking for his true talent to be recognized. But, as another of our maverick artists, Quentin Crisp, was fond of saying: 'Make no effort to join society. Stay right where you are and wait for society to form around you. Because it most certainly will.' After 30 years of persecution for his sexuality and flamboyant attire, Crisp published his memoirs and transformed from social pariah to celebrity author and monologist.

Perhaps, rarest of all – rising through the noise of mediocrity like the ethereal high note of a theremin – are those who remain unclassifiable: sublimely bonkers one-of-a-kinds. It is with a final doff of the cap that we celebrate the bittersweet Dadaist songs of Ivor Cutler, the Saturnalian jazz musician Sun Ra and Professor Stanley Unwin, whose unique career came through speaking his own made-up language, Basic Engly Twenty Fido.

2:01

MOONDOG

The New York Viking

In the late 1940s, a tall bearded blind man, dressed as a Norse god, appeared on the corner of 6th Avenue and 54th Street in midtown New York. Calling himself Moondog (but also acquiring the moniker of 'The Viking of 6th Avenue'), he cut a striking figure in a time when even collar-length hair for men would have been considered shocking. There he remained for over 25 years, becoming as familiar a New York landmark as the Empire State Building. 'Moondog's Corner' was even cited in many guidebooks of the time as a local attraction.

Sporting a cape and horned leather cap and brandishing a 6-foot spear, the Viking could be found at his post eight hours a day, most days of the year. The street was his stage. Here he'd be found playing a drum, selling poetry and sheet music or dispensing philosophy. Other times, he would just stand erect, silent and imposing, only breaking his statuesque pose to take a drink from a hollowed moose horn that hung round his neck. When asked where he was from, Moondog would reply: Sasnak ('Kansas' backwards).

To most onlookers, the Viking was a homeless eccentric. Few would have believed him to be a serious and world-renowned musician who had worked with pioneering composers Philip Glass and Steve Reich, found admirers in the likes of Leonard Bernstein and had his songs recorded by Julie Andrews.

Moondog was born Louis Thomas Hardin, in Kansas in 1916, to a religious family with a passion for the arts and culture. A love of music came to Hardin at a young age after he attended Native American sun dance rituals. The beats and polyrhythms of the music would leave an indelible mark on his own future compositions. After losing his sight in a farming accident, Hardin found increasing solace in music and, at Iowa's School for the Blind, made the decision to becoming a great composer. Penniless but ambitious, Hardin relocated to New York. Figuring that the best place to be noticed by eminent musicians was close to Carnegie Hall, he set himself up near to the entrance. While enjoying the attention and interest in his music, Hardin became deeply irritated that his unconventionally long hair and beard often brought comparisons to Jesus.

Having rejected Christianity in favour of Norse mythology, he figured that, if anything, he'd rather be mistaken for a Viking. Thus, he adopted the horns and cape and changed his name to Moondog, after a childhood pet.

Moondog's talent as a musician didn't go unnoticed by passers-by. A tiny independent record label called SMC released a few singles and EPs of his work during the late 1940s and 1950s. Leonard Bernstein was among several leading composers and conductors who regularly invited him into Carnegie Hall to observe rehearsals of the New York Philharmonic. A few even offered to help him with his career, although it always came with a caveat: lose the Viking apparel. Moondog refused, preferring to take his eccentricity further. He began to build and play his own instruments, and could now be found hunched over odd-looking zithers, triangular harps and drums, which he gave such names as *uni*, *trimba*, *tuji* and the *oo*.

THE BIRTH OF ROCK 'N' ROLL

In the early 1950s, a curious thing happened. A popular and prominent Cleveland-based DJ, Alan Freed, became obsessed with Moondog's second single, 'Moondog Symphony'. Freed renamed his show, *Moondog House*, gave himself the moniker, 'King of the Moondoggers' and even put on an event in Cleveland Arena called the Moondog Coronation Ball. In 1954, with the help of fans and musician Benny Goodman, Moondog took out an injunction against Freed and was awarded $6,000 in damages. Freed, no longer permitted to use Moondog's name, renamed his radio programme *The Rock 'n' Roll Show*, thus coining a phrase that would come to define a whole musical movement of the 20th century. The question is, if Moondog had lost the court case, would Joan Jett have had to sing, 'I love Moondogging, so put another dime in the jukebox, baby'?

Leading composers and conductors often invited Moondog to Carnegie Hall to listen to rehearsals of the New York Philharmonic.

Throughout the 1950s, Moondog's recorded output increased and his fame grew. He performed with Lenny Bruce, was befriended by Marlon Brando and Charlie Parker, and his songs were covered by Janis Joplin and Julie Andrews. For a year, he was invited to live with Philip Glass, spending much of his time jamming with Glass and Steve Reich, both of whom would go on to cite him as a major influence on the minimalist movement. By 1969, his first fully orchestrated album, *Moondog*, was released by Columbia, followed two years later by *Moondog 2*.

Despite his loathing of conventionality, Moondog's music had little in common with the arch, atonal minimalism of many of his contemporaries – nor did it follow the 4/4 beats of rock and roll. Instead, Moondog infused his music with what he named

Snake Time, preferring the jaunty swing of a 7/4 or 5/4 time signature (think of the *Mission Impossible* theme tune).

On his records, you'll also find spoken word, city sounds, jazz, choral voices and, occasionally, the howl of a dog. One track includes a duet for the whistle of an ocean liner and a bamboo flute. At a time when many composers were studiously trying to remove rhythm and melody from their own music, Moondog knew how to groove. Stationed at his corner on 6th Avenue decade after decade, he had become the axis on which New York turned.

'I'M NOT GOING TO DIE IN 4/4 TIME'

It's likely that Moondog might have remained on the streets of New York for another 25 years had it not been for an invitation to perform in Europe. While in Germany hitch-hiking one late December (and yes, still dressed as a Viking), he was picked up by a 24-year-old German archeology student, Iloner Sommer. She took a shine to him and persuaded her family to allow Moondog to stay with them for a few days over Christmas.

A few days turned out to be a 25-year residency. Sommer quit being a student and became Moondog's agent, publisher and right-hand woman, even persuading him to swap his horns for a beanie. Moondog remained in Germany for the rest of his life, free to compose and publish music, his lifelong dream realized.

Unimpeded by a need to earn a crust, his compositions got ever grander. One, a thousand-bar composition, *Tree Tone*, remains unperformed, requiring a minimum of eight conductors. Another, *Cosmos*, which required over 1,000 musicians and singers, has yet to be performed live.

In 1971, shortly before his unexpected move to Germany, Moondog moved his busking spot from 6th Avenue to Madison Avenue. Why? It was opposite the HQ of his record label, Columbia. A blind Viking signed to their label would be difficult for record company executives to ignore or forget if he was busking outside their offices every day. It epitomized Moondog's singular and canny approach to life. You have to doff your horned helmet to him. DB

2:02

Stanley Unwin standing, with the aid of an inflatable duck, in the swimming pool at the Dolphin Square apartments, London. He is dressed as a waiter, carrying glasses of beer. *Goodlilode Brewflade* translates as 'excellent beer'.

STANLEY UNWIN

Inventor of Basic Engly Twenty Fido

'Mr Unwin, what do you make of Elvis Presley?'
'Well, from across the herring-pole where harth the people has produced some waspwaist and swivel-hippy,
I must say the rhythm contrapole sideways with the head and tippy tricky half fine on the strings.'
–Stanley Unwin, *Rotatey Diskers* (1961)

So began a typical conversation with Professor Stanley Unwin, a genuine one-off in the entertainment world. His catchphrase 'deep joy' not only summed up the delight he brought to others through his verbal dexterity, but reflected the sheer radiance of the man himself.

Even if the name Stanley Unwin is unfamiliar, chances are you've seen (or heard) him through cameos in Carry On and Norman Wisdom films, his role of the Chancellor in *Chitty Chitty Bang Bang* (1968) and his innumerable appearances on TV and radio.

Unwin was, in his own words, '**a masterlode of the verbally thrips oratory**'. He created, and spoke, 'Basic Engly Twenty Fido' (Unwinese, to others). It was his own playfully knotted version of the English language – full of tongue twisters and malapropisms, and originally invented to entertain his own children.

Unwin begin working as a sound engineer for the BBC in the late 1940s. After amusing his colleagues with wordplay, he was persuaded to make a spoof sports documentary for radio. A fan letter from his heroine, comedian Joyce Grenfell, encouraged Unwin to do more. One radio appearance led to another and by the 1960s, Unwin was regularly popping up in films, TV and as a novelty guest on panel shows. He recorded an album, *Rotatey Diskers* (1961), and in 1967 was asked by the Small Faces to narrate the story of 'Happiness Stan', which takes up the whole of side two of their number-one album, *Ogdens' Nut Gone Flake* (1968). The opening is classic Unwinese:

> 'Are you all sitty comforty bolt two square on your botty?
> Then I'll begin. Like all real-life experience story this also begins once upon a polly-ti-to. Now after little lapse of time Stan became deep hungry in his tumload. After all he struggly trickly half several mileode, and anyone would suffer under this.'

When in full flow, Unwin's language has a lyrical beauty akin to Lewis Carroll's 'Jabberwocky' and Ivor Cutler's *A Stuggy Pren*. While also drawing comparisons to other 'cock-eyed' languages, such as Anthony Burgess's Nadsat in *A Clockwork Orange*, it has to be remembered that, for the most part, Unwin wasn't carefully penning his language but improvising on the spot. Where most comedians are applauded for their razor wit and one-liners, Unwin was capable of delivering a humorous monologue on any given subject while simultaneously delivering it in Unwinese – a talent that remains unparalleled.

Unwin's vocal dexterity even extended to bird song. He was able to mimic the call of a blackbird so accurately that it often drew the birds to him.

76

Unwin's most surprising role came in 1969 as the puppet lead in *The Secret Service*, a new Supermarionation production from *Thunderbirds* creator Gerry Anderson. The programme featured a puppet 'Father Unwin' as a parish priest moonlighting as a secret agent. In his daring missions he is accompanied by sidekick Matthew, who is often (and often pointlessly) shrunk and popped in Unwin's suitcase using a special gadget called 'the minimizer'.

Inevitably, it is Unwinese that helps the pair get out of scrapes. In one storyline they are flying important medical supplies over Africa when they are forced to make an emergency landing. In a rather un-PC twist, the natives turn out to be cannibals and pop the pair in a cooking pot until Father Unwin tries a bit of Unwinese. To his relief, they understand him and he sweet-talks the hungry natives into having a veggie curry that night instead.

Sadly, we'll never know how many storylines Gerry Anderson could have successfully teased out of Unwinese; *Secret Service* was pulled after the first series by the BBC, whose controller found Father Unwin 'confusing', thus missing the point entirely.

Unwin continued to make TV and radio appearances for over five decades, and was still performing into his late eighties. He was never lost for words, whether explaining microchip technology to a chatshow host or recounting the story of *The Pedy Pipeload of Hamling* for radio. He is a vital reminder of how sometimes, with a dollop of luck and good grace, the things we do for the sheer fun of it can become our vocations.

Unwin died in 2002. His gravestone bears the epitaph: 'Re-unitey in the heavenly-bode. Deep Joy!'

Sadly, the secret of his language went with him to the grave. Should you, however, ever find yourself in a parallel universe where Unwinese is the primary language, 'goodly mordlow', 'muchly grattiplude' and 'deep joy' should help you along nicely. DB

2:03

BARONESS ELSA VON FREYTAG-LORINGHOVEN

The woman who was the future

In the year 2027 it will be 100 years since the death of the poet, painter, sculptor and performance artist Baroness Elsa von Freytag-Loringhoven. By the time of this anniversary, her life will be widely celebrated. This has to be a good thing because it certainly wasn't celebrated during the 20th century.

Baroness Elsa was wild. She wore cakes for hats, postage stamps for make-up and a bra made from two tomato cans and green string. Over a 100 years before Lady Gaga turned up at the MTV Awards wearing a meat dress, the Baroness was genuinely shocking. She lived in abject poverty and was repeatedly arrested for offences ranging from theft to public nudity. She is now recognized as the first American Dada artist, although it might be more accurate to think of her as the first New York punk – 60 years too early.

She was born Else Hildegard Plötz in 1874 in Swinemünde, Pomerania, a province that's now in Poland but was then part of the German Empire. In her formative years she worked as a chorus girl, was hospitalized with syphilis, and had numerous marriages and affairs particularly with gay, impotent or cross-dressing men. She increasingly moved in avant-garde art circles and made her way to New York, where a short-lived marriage to Baron Leopold von Freytag-Loringhoven gave her a title. It was then that she met the father of conceptual art, Marcel Duchamp.

The Baroness adored Duchamp. In many ways, they were polar opposites; he was intellectual, cold and analytical and she was a wild, crazed outpouring of creative fire. He may have refused her offers of a physical relationship, but he did recognize her importance as an artist. 'The Baroness is not a Futurist,' he said, 'she is the future.'

In 1917, Duchamp entered a urinal into an exhibition held by the New York Society of Independent Artists. The society aimed to exhibit every work of art submitted, so Duchamp was challenging them to accept that the urinal, named *Fountain*, was indeed a work of art. Duchamp declared that *Fountain* was a 'readymade', a concept he first described in 1915. A readymade was a found object, he said, not made by the artist but which became a work of art because an artist declared it to be one. This raised the thorny question as to whether an artist declaring something to be art was sufficient for that object to actually be a work of art.

This was ground zero for the world of conceptual art, where art was understood to reside more in the idea than in the craft or execution of the artwork – and *Fountain* was the archetypal example of conceptual art. In the year 2000, a BBC poll of 500 experts declared that *Fountain* was the most influential work of art in the 20th century. But, back in 1917, the judges of the exhibition were less impressed. They refused to accept the urinal and most likely threw it out with the trash.

Duchamp left the art world a few years later and dedicated his life to the game of chess. But the reputation of *Fountain* continued to grow, and by the 1950s a new generation of American artists began to champion his art. Little of his early work survived at this point, but the art world is not a place to let problems like that stand in the way of making money. Duchamp was persuaded to produce a number of editions of his earlier readymades, including *Fountain*. He produced 17 new versions, many of which can now be found in the leading galleries of the world. They tend to be exhibited in Perspex cases, after a considerable number of **art students attempted to 'engage with the art'**.

One such artist was musician and producer Brian Eno who, in 1993, said, 'somebody should piss in that thing, to sort of bring it back to where it belonged. So I decided it had to be me.' He turned up at the Museum of Modern Art in New York with galvanized wire and some clear plastic tubing stuffed down his trousers then, when the guard's back was turned, poked the tube through a slot in the display case and merrily emptied his bladder.

THE PLOT THICKENS

In the early 1980s, a letter emerged, written in 1917 from Duchamp to his sister. In it he remarked how a 'female friend' had sent him a urinal as an artwork. The identity of this female friend was a mystery, and not one the art world seemed in a particular hurry to solve – until Canadian academic Irene Gammel began piecing together the story of Baroness Elsa. The Baroness was a woman entirely missing from published accounts of modernism, but who could be repeatedly glimpsed in diary entries, avant-garde magazines and letters from the time. The result was a portrait of a gifted, difficult, phenomenally original individual, who was so far ahead of the curve that she was dismissed as crazy by those who failed to understand what it was that she was doing.

Thanks to Gammel's work, we now know enough about Baroness Elsa's life and work to confidently identify her as the female friend in Duchamp's letter. *Fountain* is tonally more in keeping with her confrontational style than the dry, analytical work of Duchamp. Toilets and divinity were often linked in her work, which points back to her abusive father mocking her religious mother's prayer as her daily ablutions.

Furthermore, the urinal was submitted to the exhibition under the fictitious name of R. Mutt from Philadelphia, and the Baroness was in Philadelphia at the time. In her native German, 'R. Mutt' becomes a joke on *Armut*, referring to 'poverty' or intellectual poverty, which fits with the Baroness' opinion of the American art world's reaction to the outbreak of the First World War. Duchamp had claimed that he obtained the urinal from J.L. Mott Ironworks on 5th Avenue, but research has since shown that this could not be true, as they did not sell the correct model of urinal.

The Baroness was producing readymades as early as 1913, years before Duchamp named and intellectualized the process. There are even other examples of the Baroness taking a piece of plumbing equipment in 1917, giving it an archetypal name, declaring it to be art and then having that work credited to a better-known male artist. A plumber's trap she called *God*, for example, was misattributed to Morton Schamberg.

There is now little doubt that the most influential work of art of the 20th century was the work of Baroness Elsa von Freytag-Loringhoven, and that she sent the urinal to Duchamp in New York so that he could enter into the exhibition under an assumed name. This might make those who have invested considerable sums in one of Duchamp's 17 editions of *Fountain* nervous, but it shouldn't do. For, as Duchamp himself pointed out, it is the Baroness who is the future. JH

QUENTIN CRISP

The man who lived without shame

In his book *A Liar's Autobiography* (1980), Monty Python member Graham Chapman recounts his experience on a TV chat show in the mid-1970s when he spoke candidly about his homosexuality. A week later, the Pythons received an angry letter from a female viewer. Not only was she disgusted with Chapman but she (wrongly) believed he had chosen not to disclose his full identity. John Cleese, having gleefully volunteered to reply to the letter, thanked her for informing the Pythons that they had a homosexual in their midst and concluded that, having discovered who it was, they had been forced to kill him.

Tolerance towards homosexuality remains a work in progress for every single country around the world. Some have come further than others: in 2000, the Netherlands became the first country to legalize same-sex marriages and since then over 20 countries have followed suit. Back in the 1930s, however, one would have needed incredible courage to live as a homosexual without fear or shame in London.

Quentin Crisp lived for 35 years in the same bedsit, which he refused to ever clean.

This was the world a young Quentin Crisp strutted into – decked out in flamboyant clothes, nail polish, dyed long hair and lipstick. He had, in society's eyes, everything to be ashamed of.

Growing up as Denis Pratt in suburban Surrey, he had been a target for scorn and persecution from an early age. 'In England, sex was not popular until the permissive society began. My appearance put me apart from the rest of humanity,' he would later write. But after moving to London, Crisp began a crusade: to show the world what and who he was. And he would never deny or hide it.

> 'I laid it out so everyone could know what they were getting. If it causes no stir it covers no ground. Persistence is your greatest weapon. Once the public get bored with homosexuality, freedom will be here. I wanted to outlive the stir, teach that people like me had to go on living.'
> *–The Naked Civil Servant* (1975)

It was far from easy. In 1939, he was rejected by the army for 'suffering from sexual perversions'. He was even rejected from underground gay clubs on account of his appearance. Here regulars dressed 'straight' to look inconspicuous. If these clubs had been raided by the police, Crisp's effeminate attire would have given the game away. He was a complete outsider, on the receiving end of verbal and physical abuse almost daily.

From the 1930s to the 1960s, Crisp drifted around central London. His appearance made it almost impossible to find regular work. For a time he tried his hand as a male prostitute but, by his own admission, wasn't very good at it. He finally found his niche modelling for art classes, which he went on to do for 30 years, admitting, 'Exhibitionism is a drug; you get hooked.'

Crisp did, however, possess a Wildean wit, a flair for writing and a unique philosophy – cultivated through his own observations of humanity. 'Never try and keep up with the Joneses. Drag them down to your level. It's much cheaper,' he once quipped. In living for over 35 years in the same bedsit, which he never once cleaned. 'Don't waste your life cleaning,' comes his advice in *The Naked Civil Servant* (1975). 'After four years the dust doesn't get any thicker, it's just a question of not losing your nerve.'

In 1968, Crisp's candid autobiography, *The Naked Civil Servant*, was published by Jonathan Cape. The *Guardian* review described it as, 'the triumph of the resolute individual against the faceless multitude'. Crisp's mannered delivery, barbed wit and insights made him an excellent interviewee. A few years later, John Hurt played him in a TV adaptation of his memoir, which was met with equal praise. Crisp had moved from social pariah to celebrity.

While his life was never without friendship or a party to attend, Crisp spent most of it living alone and without a partner. He was perceived by some as a lonely, passive figure. There was certainly a cruel paradox in his own self-defeating narrative about seeking the love of a 'real man', who he referred to as his 'great dark man'. As such a man would never want to be with an effeminate homosexual, Crisp reasoned, he was doomed never to find love. Like Groucho's famously self-deprecating quote, the great dark man would not want to belong to a club that would have Crisp as a member.

Throughout the 1970s, Crisp became increasingly popular for his one-man shows, which explored his themes of lifestyle, society and individualism. In 1980, he was invited to speak in New York. The city embraced him and, at the age of 72, he decided to seek citizenship. Here was a city where everything was on display; for the first time in his life, Crisp felt that he fitted in.

While Crisp was, for many, the godfather of gay liberation, others saw him as little more than a self-hating exhibitionist. **During the 1980s,** when asked to comment on AIDS at a show in the United States he replied: 'Homosexuals are forever complaining of one ailment or another. AIDS is a fad, nothing more.' At a time of growing fear about this 'gay' disease, Crisp's reply couldn't have been more ill-timed and his refusal to apologise made him enemies (though later he would come to donate many thousands to AIDS charities).

With Enid Blyton's fondness for the word 'queer' in her Famous Five books, it seemed inevitable that her character 'Uncle Quentin' would be re-imagined as an effeminate homosexual in the Comic Strip's 1980s comedy *Five Go Mad in Dorset.*

OVERTAKEN BY THE CROWD

Crisp never lost his razor-sharp wit, sociability or transparency. Where possible, he attended every dinner party he was invited to (regardless of who his hosts were), kept his number in the New York phone book and spoke at length with anyone who called, always answering the phone with the same question: 'Oh yes?' If it was a nuisance caller, threatening him with violence, Crisp would often say, 'Would you like to make an appointment? I'm free next Tuesday.'

Crisp's great act of subversion was to be himself. In an age of conformity and conservatism, he adhered to his own code of individualism and lived long enough to see society come round to his way of thinking. He witnessed the rise of the pink pound and gay rights and was even invited back to England in the 1990s as a guest for the BBC programme *Gaytime TV*.

What Crisp didn't anticipate was that society's attitudes to homosexuality would, ultimately, overtake him. By the time he reached America, his effeminate style was passé in the gay scene. While Crisp's crusade had been to 'bore' society into accepting gay culture, he never imagined gay culture could also be hosting the party that he once saw his kind excluded from.

Crisp continued to perform into his eighties, even playing Queen Elizabeth I in the film *Orlando* (1992). In 2009, he was immortalized by lute-loving Sting in the song 'Englishman in New York' and, in the film of the same name, John Hurt returned after a 34-year hiatus to play Crisp in his autumn years.

At the end of *The Naked Civil Servant* film, Crisp is being goaded by a gang of young boys in the street. Unperturbed, he minces through them with the parting words, 'You cannot touch me now, I am one of the stately homos of England.' As a figurehead for the underdog, misfit and outcast, Quentin Crisp remains untouchable. DB

86

2:05

ALEXANDER SCRIABIN

The composer who could destroy planets

Many musicians dream of international renown; few achieve it. Even fewer dream of creating a week-long event that will cause the world to dissolve in bliss; a grandiose religious synthesis of all the arts that will herald the birth of a new world. Enter Alexander Scriabin.

Scriabin was born into an aristocratic family in Moscow. His mother, a concert pianist, died when he was one. A precocious child, he became so fascinated with pianos that he began building them, giving them away to house guests.

As an adult, he was just over 5 feet (1.5 metres) tall, effeminate, weak and supremely arrogant. Family members were embarrassed by his weird behaviour and mannerisms. His intense character and narcissism caused many to dislike him. He claimed to be the apotheosis of world creation: 'I am the aim of aims, the end of ends.' He also famously said, 'I am God.' Being born on Christmas Day reinforced this belief and he once tried to walk on Lake Geneva and preach to the fishermen.

Scriabin was curious about the world, reading Schopenhauer and Nietzsche and filling notebooks with philosophical musings. In his twenties, he achieved celebrity and influence. He performed his own piano works to positive reviews, toured in Russia and abroad, and established his reputation as a composer.

COLOURFUL SOUNDSCAPES

In the early 1900s, things started to get interesting. Scriabin was affected by synaesthesia and associated colours with the tones of his atonal scale. His chromatic harmony created a richness, complexity and emotional expression that he found frightening; he couldn't play his own Sonata No. 6 in public, finding it 'nightmarish, murky, unclean, and mischievous'.

In his last symphony, *Prometheus: The Poem of Fire*, he projected synchronized colours using a *tastiera per luce*, or 'keyboard of lights', which glowed along with particular notes. The keyboard was multi-coloured, but the lights themselves were a little basic.

Preparation for the Final Mystery was to be Scriabin's master work, intended to bring together all he had learned about philosophy, synaesthesia, Theosophy and poetry. He thought of his music as fragments of this mystical vision – as bridges to the beyond in the tradition of composers such as Wagner and Stockhausen, who wanted their music to bring about 'aesthetic, social, or cosmic apocalypse'.

Scriabin delved heavily into Russian symbolism and Theosophy, and his notebooks are filled with fascinating passages charting his personal voyage. He believed he could attain the Symbolist ideal of art having a material effect upon reality, by channelling divine energy through the careful coordination of elements designed to stimulate multiple sensations.

He started working on *The Mysterium* in 1903, but it remained incomplete when he died in 1915. His vision comprised a seven-day mega-work with dirigibles and bells suspended from clouds that would summon spectators from all over the world. A reflecting pool of water would complete the divinity of the half-circle stage, with spectators sitting in tiers across the water and the least spiritually advanced in the balconies. Seating would radiate from the stage, where Scriabin would sit at the piano surrounded by a host of instruments, singers and dancers. The cast would include an orchestra, dancers, a choir and costumed speakers articulating rhythmic texts in processions.

The work required special people, special artists and a completely new culture. The entire group would be permeated continually by movement. Together with fellow Theosophist Emile Sigogne, Scriabin worked on a new language for *The Mysterium*, which had Sanskritic roots but also included cries, interjections, exclamations and sounds of breath. The temple in which the event would take place would not be made of one type of stone but would continually change with the atmosphere and motion of the piece. This would be done with the aid of mists and lights, which would modify the architectural contours; sunrises would be preludes and sunsets codas; flames would erupt in shafts of light and sheets of fire and constantly changing lighting effects would pervade the cast and audience, each to number in the thousands. The choreography would include glances, eye motions, touching of hands, odours of both pleasant perfumes and acrid smokes. Furthermore, the whole world would be invited: 'animals, insects, birds, all must be there.'

Scriabin intended that the first (and only) performance would be held in the Himalayan foothills in a half-temple that would crumble due to the vibrations and open the ritual to the heavens. The event would annihilate space and melt reality, bringing about the end of the world and replacing humankind with nobler beings. All participants would dematerialize, allowing them to achieve spiritual unity with the divine cosmos.

Fortunately for the human race, in 1915 Scriabin nicked a boil on his upper lip when shaving and **died from septicaemia at the age of 43**. His funeral was attended by such numbers that tickets had to be issued. Rachmaninoff went on tour, playing only Scriabin's music, and the composer was acknowledged as one of the essential voices of the early 20th century. TG

At the time of his death, Scriabin had sketched 72 pages of the prelude to *The Mysterium*, entitled *Prefatory Action*. Composer Alexander Nemtin spent 28 years reforming this sketch into a three-hour-long work, which was eventually recorded. You can have a listen at *bit.ly/ErnestMysterium*

SUN RA

The jazz musician from Saturn

At the beginning of the 1974 film *Space is the Place*, a twin tadpole-like spaceship floats through the cosmos while a strident female voice chants: 'It's after the end of the world, don't you know that yet?' The scene moves to Saturn, where strange jellyfish-like plants float in the air and a man, magnificently attired in Egyptian robes and headdress, addresses a death-like figure:

'The music is different here, the vibrations are different, not like Planet Earth. We'll set up a colony for black people. We'll bring them here through isotopic teleportation, transmolecularization, or, better still, teleport the whole planet through music.'

It's a suitable entry point as any into the cosmic world of Sun Ra, a musician and philosopher who created extraordinary, unearthly music and preferred not to think of himself as a man but an angel from Saturn. Throughout his life, Sun Ra was on a mission – to raise planetary consciousness. His music became the means and the message was 'to initiate a discourse on otherness'. His mission statement in a 1967 pamphlet read:

'To perform spiritual-cosmic-intergalactic-infinity research works relative to worlds-dimensions-planes in galaxies and universes beyond the present now known used imagination of mankind, beyond the intergalactic central sun and works relative to spiritual advancement of our presently known world.'

But while Sun Ra sometimes rhapsodized about a utopian future, for him humanity was already damned; its true salvation lay in space exploration and **leaving the planet for somewhere better** (ideally, Saturn).

Sun Ra was only the second person in US history to report an encounter with alien beings.

91

Growing up during the 1920s and 1930s in Birmingham, Alabama – known at the time as the most segregated city in the world – it's no surprise that Sun Ra lost faith in a species that insisted every race in his home town had to have their own shopping day. Instead, he became fascinated with cosmology, Egyptology and science fiction. And while always claiming to be interested in science fact, not fiction, both would ultimately inform his work.

MUSIC TO ASTOUND PEOPLE

Sun Ra began performing in swing bands in the 1930s but soon began to move away from conventional jazz. By the 1960s, his style was fully formed – a unique and exhilarating blend of free jazz, big band swing, exotic costumes, sci-fi-inspired album artwork, Egyptian symbology and pioneering electronic sounds.

While at college, Sun Ra converted his living space into a rehearsal room. This would be a template for the rest of his life – over the years his home became a recording studio, record label and the living quarters for **Arkestra**, his band of dedicated followers, many of whom claimed he had special powers. In living with Sun Ra, Arkestra had to abide by his strict house rules: no alcohol, drugs or women could be brought into the house. Those who broke the rules would forfeit a solo the next time the band performed.

His band were also known, at various times, as Myth Science Arkestra, Omniverse Arkestra, Cosmocentric Arkestra and Intergalactic Research Arkestra.

What performances they were! Sun Ra's live shows were like nothing that had come before – incorporating dance, theatre and costume. The performers would often go on stage chanting 'Heigh-ho, heigh-ho, it's off to work we go', dressed in space-age costumes replete with flashing lights and propellors. Sun Ra would sit behind his keyboard, centre stage in a shimmering cape and elaborate Egyptian headgear. No show was ever the same. 'I play music that will astound people,' he told the world. 'But they need to be astounded and shook up before it's too late.'

It did, however, get a little silly at times. After a midget Darth Vader began to appear on stage for a lightsaber duel with an alien creature, someone owed it to Sun Ra to slip a copy of *Spinal Tap* under his bedroom door.

At the end of the film *Space is the Place*, Sun Ra leaves Earth shortly before we see the planet destroy itself, engulfed in a fireball. Sun Ra has a small crew on board his ship, ready to start life afresh on Saturn. Viewers are left to digest an epic biblical tale of caution in which Sun Ra appears to play both the Old Testament God and Noah. It is here, perhaps, that we reach the unique essence of Sun Ra. While the likes of Alice Cooper and David Bowie played with alter egos in their live shows and on record, Sun Ra took it to another realm entirely.

'I do not come to you as a reality; I come to you as the myth, because that's what black people are. Myths. I came from a dream that the black man dreamed a long time ago. I'm actually a presence sent to you by your ancestors.'
–*Space is the Place* (1974)

In changing his name and claiming to be from Saturn, Sun Ra had (in his own words) become a 'living myth'. He embodied a narrative that mixed science fiction, Egyptian symbology and the (inevitable) destruction of Earth, with himself at the centre as the saviour. It was a curiously similar story to that created by Oberto Airaudi, founder of the Damanhur community in Italy (see Chapter 5). If myths spring up from our collective unconscious, as psychologist Carl Jung believed, could it be that both men, despite being from different races, countries and times, were channelling a new myth for the late 20th century?

Sun Ra never faltered in his mythic role. In his seventies, admitted to hospital with a stroke, he was asked for his address: 'Saturn', came the stock reply. He died in 1993 but Arkestra lives on, touring his cosmic sounds around the globe, attired in their glittering robes.

With over 200 albums to his name, knowing where to enter the rich waters of Sun Ra's music can be problematic. His six decades of compositions range from big band swing and Disney covers to raucous outbursts of free jazz that could set your teeth on edge. It's best to dive in with the opening 21-minute title track from *Space is the Place*. From here, keep swimming. The water will get turbulent at times, but then it is Saturnalian water, after all. DB

RE/
SEARCH

2:07

PEOPLE SERIES:
Volume
One

BOB FLANAGAN:

SUPERMASOCHIST

BOB FLANAGAN

The man who fought pain with pain

There comes a time in every young man's life when he wonders what it might be like to have a beautiful stranger nail his penis to a two-by-four. What thoughts would rush through his head as the blunt iron nib pressed into the soft flesh of his cock and the hammer was raised in anticipation? With beads of sweat trickling down his chest, more fear now than man, would he scream out? Would he call the whole thing off, knowing it would condemn him to a life of uncertainty? Or would he find the calm and courage within himself to meet his assailant's eyes, nod his assent, and in the moment just before the blow is struck recall what Melville wrote about the hunt for Moby Dick: 'You bid adieu to circumspect life and only exist in a delirious throb.'

Artist, writer and celebrated 'supermasochist' Bob Flanagan – best known for the performance piece *Nailed* (1989), which ended with his flaccid, bleeding penis nailed to a board – is one of the few among us who has lived a life that throbbed with immediacy. Flanagan's was a life in which fears were not only confronted, they were swallowed whole; a life in which each day declared: alive and not dead.

Flanagan was born in New York on 26 December 1952. He was diagnosed with cystic fibrosis, a congenital disease that causes an overproduction of mucus in the lungs and pancreas. People with cystic fibrosis have chronic lung problems and severe ongoing digestive issues, and most are infertile. There is no known cure and, in the 1950s, children born with the condition rarely made it past early childhood. Doctors predicted that the young Flanagan would be dead in ten years. When he passed away in 1996, he was 43 and one of the longest-living survivors of the disease at the time. How did he manage to defy the odds and live to this relatively ripe old age?

A strict regimen of respiratory massage therapy, antibiotic drugs, ventilators and nipple clamps. Spanking too, and piercing, coupled with some light knife play. Masochism was, from an early age, Flanagan's means of gaining control and ownership over a body that was constantly breaking down and being handed over to medical professionals to pump, prod and prick into a semblance of health. Ultimately, he would progress to suspension and self-carpentry, but in the beginning, as a young boy, he would settle for autoerotic-asphyxiation and a little light whipping, alone in his suburban bedroom.

'A COMPLEX MAN'

Writing was Flanagan's other great vice and, although he dropped out of his literature degree early, poetry paved the way for his later career as a performance artist. At Los Angeles literary arts centre Beyond Baroque, he found his people and his vocation. Here, Flanagan finally felt comfortable enough among its punk poets (Dennis Cooper), musicians (the band X), and artists (Mike Kelley) to come out as a masochist, confiding in his friend Cooper, and turning to sadomasochism as a subject in his poetry.

Of course, behind every great man is a woman with a branding iron and a ball gag, and Flanagan wouldn't have become who he was without the contribution of Sheree Rose, his life partner and stage collaborator for 14 years. They met at Beyond Baroque and began performing their double act – starting with a pretty tame show that saw Rose throwing food at Flanagan in a gimp mask and escalating to the infamous *Nailed*.

After that, Bob blew up. Nine Inch Nails and Danzig got him to perform in their music videos; Rose was featured in the ground-breaking *Modern Primitives* (1989) anthology and Flanagan got his own book, *Bob Flanagan: Supermasochist* (1993), which became a kind of bible for fellow cystic fibrosis sufferers. People also started to think about Flanagan and Rose's work together with that of other body artists such as Orlan and Franko B who, with increasingly shocking shows, encouraged their audiences to think about the ways that culture sanitizes images of the dirty, sick or abnormal body.

Flanagan and Rose's performances had more humour and

self-awareness than many other po-faced examples, however. One memorable routine, featured in Kirby Dick's beautiful and harrowing 1997 documentary *Sick: The Life and Death of Bob Flanagan, Supermasochist*, begins with Flanagan singing the words, 'Supermasochistic Bob has cystic fibrosis' to the rousing tune of 'Supercalifragilistic':

'When he was born the doctors said he had
this bad disease
That gave him awful stomach-aches
and made him cough and wheeze
Any normal person
would've buckled from the pain
But SuperBob got twisted, now
he's into whips and chains
I'm dili-dili, I'm gonna die
I'm dili-dili, I'm gonna die...'

'Bob was a complex man,' his friend Dennis Cooper remembers in *Flanagan's Wake* (1996), 'who wanted simultaneously to be Andy Kaufman, Harry Houdini, David Letterman, John Keats and a character out of a de Sade novel'. He was also – and Flanagan would probably appreciate the irreverence – a Christlike figure whose incredible suffering, endured and inflicted, is an example to us all. DH

EDITH SITWELL

The world's first white rapper

On the front cover of 1971 Penguin paperback *English Eccentrics*, there is a portrait of a woman with a nose like a hawfinch's beak, high-arching painted brows and a black turban knotted on the top of her forehead. Her gaze is fixed to the floor; lash-less, heavy-lidded eyes almost closed; jewelled hands clasped to her chest.

The photograph was taken by Cecil Beaton and the model was Edith Sitwell, author of the book that describes our nation's weirder figures, from ornamental hermits and charlatans to quacks and misers. One might think it odd for a book about famous eccentrics from history to have a portrait of the author on the cover, but on learning more about this angular-faced woman, one soon discovers that Edith Sitwell – poet, modernist and pioneer of early white rapping – was clearly an unconventional character.

Edith was the daughter of one of England's quintessential eccentrics, Sir George Sitwell. Growing up with a father who claimed to have invented a musical toothbrush and a mini revolver for shooting wasps was not as pleasurable as one might assume. 'I barely saw him,' Sitwell revealed in an interview in her later years. 'I saw far too much of my mother.' Too much of a mother who made it abundantly clear from Edith's infancy that she wasn't wanted; often inflicting bouts of unfathomable rage on her daughter and sending her to her room for 'precocious behaviour'. When asked by a family friend what she was going to be when she grew up, the four-year-old Edith replied: 'A genius.'

To grow up without a parent's love must inflict wounds that mark the course of your life, no matter how illustrious your surroundings and lineage (Edith's was born into an aristocratic family descended from the Plantagenets, and raised on a vast Derbyshire estate). Sir George showed his notion of care in his own peculiar way, attempting to 'fix' Edith's prominent nose with a clamp and her curved spine with a medieval-style corset she was forced to wear in bed. She called it her 'bastille'.

Edith managed to find some comfort in the companionship of her family's servants, in particular the butler who would covertly do his utmost to protect Edith from her parents' unpredictable tantrums. There was the occasional flicker of jollity brought by prank-playing relatives, who would place buckets of water above doors and hide live lobsters in beds. And her early childhood years by the sea in Scarborough were coloured by minstrels, pierrots, contortionists, tramps and mentally disturbed cast-offs, all of whom made an impression on the young outsider.

While Edith was wounded and baffled by the treatment she received as a child, she harnessed that angst to fuel her art. For Edith, her work was a form of religion:

> 'Poetry is the deification of reality, and one of its purposes is to show that the dimensions of man are, as Sir Arthur Eddington said, "halfway between those of an atom and a star".'
> –*Life* magazine (1963)

AN ELECTRIC EEL SET IN A POOL OF CATFISH

It wasn't until she broke away from the family home and set off for London with her governess and friend Helen Rootham in 1914 that Edith began to flourish artistically. Her gritty, satiric style flouted the bucolic Georgian poetry of the day, setting her apart even from the ubiquitous Bloomsbury Set of the 1920s, whom she sourly described as having 'civilised all their instincts away. They've civilised their senses away, too' (*Selected Letters of Edith Sitwell* edited by Richard Greene (Virago, 2007)).

She experimented with sound and rhythm in her poems, a series of which she performed in an avant-garde 'rap' with an instrumental accompaniment by William Walton. There was a political edge to her poetry, too, which she used to oppose England's role in the First World War, and later in her best-known poem 'Still Falls the Rain' (1940), about the bombing raids in Sheffield in the Second World War, and *Three Poems of the Atomic Age* (1948), based on the Hiroshima bombing.

She was instrumental in bringing Wilfred Owen's poetry to the forefront after his death and championed the works of

Dylan Thomas and W.B. Yeats, striving to seek out and publicize fresh talent wherever she saw it.

Edith – a sensitive soul – had her critics, whom she described as 'the pipsqueakery' and 'impertinent young men'. F.R. Leavis pronounced the Sitwells (Edith and her two poet brothers, Osbert and Sacheverell) as 'belonging to the history of publicity rather than of poetry' (*New Bearings in English Poetry* (1932).

The Sitwell siblings were indeed in the public eye for reasons beyond their art – the most scandalous being their mother's imprisonment for fraud in 1915 – as well as Edith's ostentatious dress sense. Edith was defiant in spite of her sensitivity; a chronicler of social injustice and campaigner against cruelty, rudeness and snobbery. In response to an interviewer asking her thoughts on her being known as 'forbidding and dangerous', she retorted, 'I don't think I'm forbidding, unless when I absolutely refuse to be taught my job by people who know nothing about it.'

While finding contentment in poetry, hosting literary salons, writing historical essays and taking jaunts to Paris and America, it's said that Edith never found love or the intimacy of a physical relationship. As one biographer put it, 'Edith was returned unopened.' She did fall in love once or twice, but her strongest emotional bond was with her live-in chum, Helen Rootham.

Perhaps it was a conscious choice not to marry and bring up children like her loveless parents, who were thrown together as teenagers. Maybe spinsterhood was all she desired. Or perhaps Edith, described by biographer Richard Greene as a 'strange combination of kindness and cruelty, courage and duplicity, simplicity and artifice' (*Edith Sitwell: Avant-garde Poet, English Genius* (2012)), simply wasn't suited to being tied down. Whatever the conclusion, in the words of Greene, 'Edith Sitwell is a poet who matters – enormously.' Essentially a victim of emotional abuse and overlooked for her artistic credibility, Edith was a modernist pioneer, a champion of new talent and one of the leading poets of the early 20th century.

And what did she have to say about being regarded as eccentric?: 'I am not an eccentric. It's just that I am more alive than most people. I am an unpopular electric eel in a pool of catfish.' (*Life* magazine, 1963). AW

IVOR CUTLER

The poet who never grew up

Somewhere in north London, a bus driver is having a bad day. His foul mood is picked up on by all of those boarding his bus. The passengers, in typical English fashion, ignore his tempestuous face and hurry along to find a seat. The last one on is a short man, sporting round spectacles, plus-fours, a tweed jacket splattered with badges and a hat decorated with a plastic sunflower. Noting the driver's countenance, the man silently reaches into a bag, pulls out a sheet of stickers and attaches one to the driver's lapel. The driver stares down at the three words on his jacket and breaks into a huge grin. The man takes his place on the bus and sits down. On the driver's lapel are the words 'You are beautiful'.

From the 1950s to the 1990s, this curious individual, Ivor Cutler, could often be seen cycling around north London, handing out his specially made 'stickies' with such aphorisms as 'You are dust', 'True happiness is knowing you are a hypocrite' and 'Women of the world take over'. Confused onlookers might even be treated to 'Never knowingly understand'.

Cutler moved to the capital from Glasgow in the 1950s to teach, but dedicated his spare time to writing strange poetry and songs, usually to the wheezy accompaniment of his portable harmonium. The sheer novelty of his words and music led to a small record deal in 1959 and the release of *Ivor Cutler of Y'hup*.

Songs such as 'Pickle Your Knees', which ends abruptly with the line 'And that's the end of my song', gave a taste of what was to follow. Over the next four decades, Cutler released a string of albums, peppered with his harmonium-drenched songs and poems. His most cherished performances are a series of twisted childhood reminiscences called *Life in a Scotch Sitting Room*, in which he recounts fictionalized tales of his family going on day trips to see a tree or, in the absence of a toilet in the house, peeing into a sponge.

Cutler's world was a unique, parallel twist on the everyday, in which the minutiae of life – from socks to micro-organisms – took on a gently surreal life of their own. It was a place where market stalls sold second-hand cups of tea, people had woollen eyes and Ivor's toe bore a hole through which he could see Australia.

In 'Fremsley' – which was, by Ivor's standards, an epic poem – Cutler befriends a sparrow who is, for reasons never explained, being pursued by an aristocrat ('a man larger than life intended') and his slavering dogs. Cutler saves Fremsley by hiding him under his T-shirt. The poem ends with the narrator taking Fremsley home and, unexpectedly, eating him for tea with chips. While his songs, such as 'Bicarbonate of Chicken', are often just plain silly, at other times there is an air of malevolence and melancholia. In the paradoxical 'I'm Happy', Cutler sings with a dark humour: 'I'm happy, I'm happy, and I'll punch the man who says I'm not.'

ALL CHILDREN ARE ARTISTS

Cutler lived in the same north London flat for 30 years, collected ivory cutlery, obsessed about botany and insects (one of his most-loved songs is a little ditty called 'I Believe in Bugs') and was a self-confessed 'unjoiner' who loathed rules and regulations. A classic outsider artist, it was his way or not at all. Cutler put his cult success down to two words, 'John Peel', and still holds the record for taking part in the most *Peel Sessions*, spanning five decades. A friendship with Lennon and McCartney led to him being cast him as Buster Bloodvessel, the bus conductor in *Magical Mystery Tour* (1967). Regrettably, Cutler's big scenes – a romantic moment on the beach with Aunt Jessie and a performance of his own song, 'I'm Going in a Field' – were later cut.

The DJ Andy Kershaw once told a story about booking Cutler for a gig at Leeds Polytechnic when he (Andy) was a student there. After tracking down Ivor's home number, he called him and offered £400 for the gig. After a long pause, Cutler replied:

'Offer me less.'
'I beg your pardon?' came Kershaw's confused reply.
'Offer me less,' Ivor repeated.
'Err, £300?' suggested Kershaw.
'Done,' said Ivor.

On the day of the gig, Ivor was invited to Andy's house for food. Sitting in the lounge eating, Ivor looked out of the window and noticed a young man furtively graffitiing a wall across the road. In his deadpan voice, he turned to Kershaw and said: 'Has he not discovered masturbation yet?' It was a typical Cutler response: mischievous and utterly unexpected.

Like Gilbert & George, Cutler's inscrutable persona was part of his art. On stage, he delivered his words and music stony-faced. Occasionally, fellow poet and partner Phyllis King would join Ivor to dust his harmonium, perform a few poems of her own or just sit in the corner, knitting. Ivor's insistence on always being addressed as Mr Cutler or that audiences clap

Ivor Cutler and
Phyllis King emerging
from a fake door at
the BBC sound
effects studio

106

at half-volume was usually met with nervous laughter. Was he serious? With the latter he was. An active member of the Noise Abatement Society, Cutler stuffed his fingers in his ears if the applause was too loud for his liking. On stage and on radio, he challenged the great taboo of silence, enjoying pauses that would have made even Harold Pinter hot under the collar. 'That silence was given to you for free,' he would conclude, after a pregnant pause.

The Zen philosopher Alan Watts once said: 'the true meaning of life is no meaning; its sense is nonsense.' Cutler, in his own way, had come to the same realization. Two of his stickies – 'Silence and space, the dark flowers of creativity', and 'Never knowingly understand', reflect his Zen approach to life. In the 1970s, he appeared in BBC documentary 'In Search of the Great English Eccentric'. When presenter Dave Allen asks: 'What are you?' Cutler replies: 'I am a child. Life is to play games.'

Cutler continued to perform and release records until his 'retirement' in 2004, at the age of 81. For those unfamiliar with his poems and songs, it pays to listen to him first. Once you've heard Cutler's lilting Glaswegian timbre, it's impossible not to read the poems without his voice in your head.

Picasso famously said: 'All children are artists. The problem is how to remain an artist once you've grown up.' Cutler, in his own inimitable way, got around the problem by making the decision to simply never grow up. DB

SEEKERS' DIRECTORY

MOONDOG

COMPILATION ALBUM *Moondog: Viking of Sixth Avenue* (2008) is a good place to start your exploration.

ALBUMS Continue with *Moondog* (1969), *Moondog 2* (1971), *H'art Songs* (1979).

FILM *The Viking of 6th Avenue* (unreleased) –
thevikingof6thavenue.com

PILGRIMAGE Take a trip to New York and stand on the corner of 6th Avenue and 54th Street.

STANLEY UNWIN

ALBUM *Rotatey Diskers with Unwin* (1960)

TV SERIES *The Secret Service* (1969)

ALBUM Small Faces, *Ogdens' Nut Gone Flake* (1968)

BARONNES ELSA VON FREYTAG-LORINGHOVEN

BOOK John Higgs, *Stranger Than We Can Imagine: Making Sense of the 20th Century* (2015)

PODCAST *Odditorium* podcast, series 1, episode 20: 'The Baroness & the Urinal' – oddpodcast.com

BIOGRAPHY Irene Gammel, *Baroness Elsa: Gender, Dada and Everyday Modernity – A Cultural Biography* (2003)

COMPILATION *Body Sweats: The Uncensored Writings of Elsa von Freytag-Loringhoven* (2001), Baronnes Elsa von Freytag-Loringhoven

QUENTIN CRISP

FILM *The Naked Civil Servant* (1975). This biopic starring John Hurt is a must-see.

FILM *An Englishman in New York* (2009). John Hurt reprises his role in a film that covers the latter years of Quentin Crisp's life spent living in Manhattan.

MONOLOGUE *An Evening with Quentin Crisp* (1980)

ALEXANDER SCRIABIN

MUSIC *Mysterium: Prefatory Action*. Alexander Nemtin spent 28 years reforming Scriabin's 72-page prelude to the *Mysterium* sketch into a three-hour-long work. You can listen to it on YouTube – Scriabin/Nemtin, bit.ly/ErnestMysterium

SUN RA

ALBUMS *Space is the Place* (1973) and *We Travel the Spaceways* (1967)

DOCUMENTARY *A Joyful Noise* (1980)

FIELD TRIP The Sun Ra Arkestra. Sun Ra's group is still touring – sunraarkestra.com

BOB FLANAGAN

DOCUMENTARY FILM *Sick: The Life and Death of Bob Flanagan Supermasochist* (1997)

BANNED MUSIC VIDEO Nine Inch Nails, *Happiness in Slavery*, Uncensored (1992)

EDITH SITWELL

BIOGRAPHY Richard Green, *Edith Sitwell: Avant-garde Poet, English Genius* (2011)

ANTHOLOGY *Edith Sitwell Collected Poems* (2006)

BOOK Edith Sitwell, *English Eccentrics* (1971)

IVOR CUTLER

DOCUMENTARY Dave Allen, *In Search of the Great English Eccentric* (1974)

ALBUMS *Dandruff* (1974), *Velvet Donkey* (1975), *Jammy Smears* (1976), *Life in a Scotch Sitting Room* (1978)

DOCUMENTARY *Archive on 4: Ivor Cutler at 90* (2015), BBC Radio 4, drbramwell.com/radio-podcasts

BOOK Ivor Cutler, *A Nice Wee Present from Scotland* (1988)

PODCAST *Odditorium* podcast, series 1, episode 24: Ivor Cutler with Sandy Grierson – oddpodcast.com

3

WILD AT HEART

WILD AT HEART

In May 2003, mountaineer Aron Ralston was presented with the ashes of something that had once been very precious to him: his right arm. The limb was cremated shortly after Ralston made world news for an inconceivable act of bravery. Descending a gully in Canyonlands National Park, Utah, Ralston dislodged an 800-pound (363kg) boulder that crushed his right arm, pinning him down so that he was unable to move. He remained trapped there for five days, sipping from a single flask of water and nibbling on the two burritos he had brought as a packed lunch. By the fourth night, delirious and severely dehydrated, Ralston carved his name and (presumed) date of death on the canyon wall only to wake the next morning with a renewed vigour and impulse to live. With a cheap pocket knife, he performed a one-hour amputation on his right arm and – a further six hours later – stumbled upon a family who helped him get to hospital. Ralston – who continues as a mountaineer – is living proof of the endurance, courage and resourcefulness that some of us are capable of in the face of adversity.

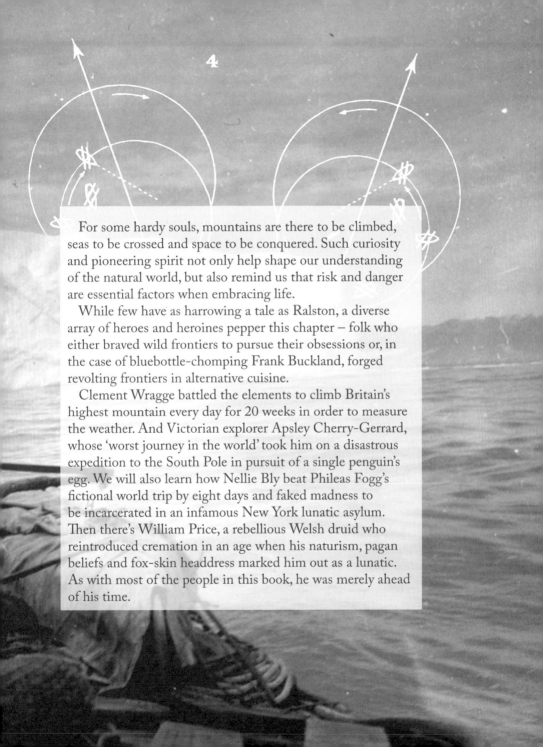

For some hardy souls, mountains are there to be climbed, seas to be crossed and space to be conquered. Such curiosity and pioneering spirit not only help shape our understanding of the natural world, but also remind us that risk and danger are essential factors when embracing life.

While few have as harrowing a tale as Ralston, a diverse array of heroes and heroines pepper this chapter – folk who either braved wild frontiers to pursue their obsessions or, in the case of bluebottle-chomping Frank Buckland, forged revolting frontiers in alternative cuisine.

Clement Wragge battled the elements to climb Britain's highest mountain every day for 20 weeks in order to measure the weather. And Victorian explorer Apsley Cherry-Gerrard, whose 'worst journey in the world' took him on a disastrous expedition to the South Pole in pursuit of a single penguin's egg. We will also learn how Nellie Bly beat Phileas Fogg's fictional world trip by eight days and faked madness to be incarcerated in an infamous New York lunatic asylum. Then there's William Price, a rebellious Welsh druid who reintroduced cremation in an age when his naturism, pagan beliefs and fox-skin headdress marked him out as a lunatic. As with most of the people in this book, he was merely ahead of his time.

3:01

FRANK BUCKLAND

The world's worst vegetarian

Ever wondered what a fly, earwig or rhinoceros might taste like? You haven't? Well perhaps that's no great surprise. Had you been alive in Victorian England during the mid-1800s, however, you just might have been caught up in a craze known as zoophagy: the practice of eating *all* animals, the more exotic the better.

Zoophagy's leading exponent was no experimental chef but a Victorian eccentric called Frank Buckland, who gave up a medical career in favour of natural history and fisheries. Not content with merely studying the animal kingdom, Buckland made it his life ambition to determine the palatability of every living creature. He encouraged others to become zoophaginists by hosting lavish dinners in which he served boiled sea slugs, antelope, fried worms, guan stew, squirrel pie, frogs, grilled parrot, roast kangaroo, ostrich, puppies, snails and soup made from the sinews of a deer.

Buckland – a stout, bearded man with butcher's arms – was often found with a creature in tow or about his person. He kept a matchbox filled with toads and a small tortoise in his pocket. When Buckland studied at Oxford, chameleons, marmots, snakes, an eagle, a jackal and a bear named Tiglath-Pileser shared his digs. Unsurprisingly, they often escaped. After moving to London, Buckland added to his menagerie a parrot, a troop of monkeys, tame mice and a jaguar. These often scarpered too – notably the monkeys, which, according to Buckland's biographer, G. Burgess, once resulted in a 'thrilling chase across the housetops of London'.

It was here in the capital that Buckland befriended members of the London Zoological Gardens; when one of the **zoo's residents died**, Buckland would be the first to be informed in case he fancied scoffing it. Such was Buckland's notoriety that a joke went around London that if he was seen walking down their street people would call in their cats, just to be on the safe side.

In May 1874, Frank Buckland gave a talk at Brighton Aquarium and served up a giant rhinoceros pie to his audience. He acquired the animal after it had passed away at a nearby zoo.

Frank inherited some of his eccentricities from his father, Reverend William Buckland. William, a noted palaeontologist, had a table at his home made from coprolite (dinosaur poo) and was prone to rushing up to students in lectures with a hyena's skull in hand, demanding they answer the question: 'What is it that rules the world?' (The answer for him was 'the stomach'.)

Darwin, it is noted, found William a distinctly vulgar individual. One famous anecdote, often attributed to both father and son, tells of an evening when William Buckland was invited to dine with Lord Harcourt, archbishop of York. After the meal, Harcourt brought out a family heirloom in a silver casket.

'Bet you can't guess what this is,' Harcourt said to Buckland, opening the casket and pointing at a shrivelled piece of flesh. Taking this as a challenge, and without a moment's hesitation, Buckland popped the thing in his mouth and swallowed. His host was horrified, Bvuckland had just gobbled up their most prized family heirloom: the heart of King Louis 14th.

There was, however, a serious intent behind Frank Buckland's eating habits – a genuine desire to make meat affordable and to broaden the diet of poor British families. A zoophany evangelist, in 1860 he help found the **Acclimatization Society of Great Britain,** one of many such groups dedicated to introducing species to new ecosystems and the domestication of exotic creatures for their meat. Members attempted to raise yak, bison, buffalo and kangaroo on their estates. Successes were short-lived but the existence of the society did give Buckland the opportunity to import a wide variety of exotic creatures.

While Buckland failed to establish zoophagy as a national pastime, he did anticipate a time when the British palate would grow tired of its traditional meat and two veg diet. In concocting dishes with snails, worms and bulls testicles, one of the UK's most celebrated chefs, Heston Blumenthal, demonstrates a growing curiosity about more exotic types of cuisine. And while serving up panther, whale or elephant to one's dinner guests would be distinctly frowned upon in these enlightened times, the garden and countryside still hold a myriad of opportunities for anyone with the curiosity (and stomach) to revive the art of zoophagy. *DB*

It was acclimatization groups that brought bumble bees to New Zealand and rabbits to Australia (which the Aussies are still angry about) and European starlings across the Atlantic to America so they could provide after-dinner entertainment.

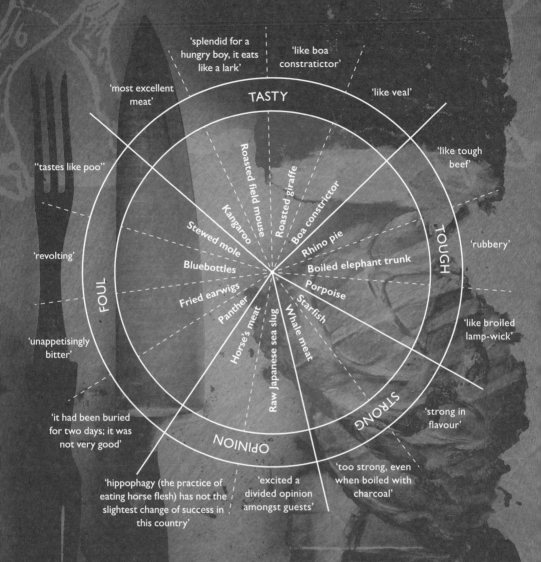

'splendid for a hungry boy, it eats like a lark'

'like boa constratictor'

'most excellent meat'

'like veal'

TASTY

'like tough beef'

"tastes like poo"

Roasted field mouse

Roasted giraffe

Boa constrictor

Kangaroo

Rhino pie

'revolting'

Stewed mole

Boiled elephant trunk

'rubbery'

FOUL

Bluebottles

Porpoise

TOUGH

Fried earwigs

Starfish

Panther

'like broiled lamp-wick'

'unappetisingly bitter'

Horse's meat

Whale meat

Raw Japanese sea slug

STRONG

'strong in flavour'

OPINION

'it had been buried for two days; it was not very good'

'hippophagy (the practice of eating horse flesh) has not the slightest change of success in this country'

'excited a divided opinion amongst guests'

'too strong, even when boiled with charcoal'

Frank Buckland's
PALATABILITY SCALE

CLEMENT WRAGGE

The notorious meteorologist and mystic

On the south-west flank of Ben Nevis's summit plateau lies a metal-lined wooden box, the size and shape of a large casket. It has stood there for over a century, marking the site of a spring but bearing the name of a person whose trajectory in life coincided, albeit briefly, with the summit of this grand Scottish mountain. The squat, fat box is called Wragge's Well and it was named after a tall, lean and peculiar man named Clement Wragge.

Clement Lindley Wragge was born in Worcestershire in 1852. He lost both parents early, and from the age of five was raised by his grandmother, who nurtured an interest in science in the young orphan. Her death forced the now 13-year-old to be moved on to an aunt in London. Initially following the family path into the law – and installed at great expense by his uncle to study at the prestigious Lincoln's Inn – at the age of 21, Wragge came into his inheritance. Feet itched by an itinerant childhood, Wragge decided to take a break from his studies for a 'brief' tour of the world. By the time he returned to England it was clear to his disappointed Uncle George that the young Clement was perhaps not a future cornerstone of the family's law firm, and it was duly confirmed: in 1876, soon after dropping out of Lincoln's Inn, Wragge enrolled as a midshipman on a sailboat bound for Australia.

Clement Wragge was interested in meteorology, and his time at sea gave him a great deal of time to observe weather systems moving through the oceanic skies. Taking a position in the South Australian Surveyor General's office, his interests advanced. A year after arriving in Australia, Wragge married the opulently named Leonora Edith Florence d'Eresby Thornton. In 1878, they returned to England where Wragge established two weather stations in Staffordshire – one low-level station at his local railway station, and one high-level station nearby, at the summit of Beacon Stoop. Wragge monitored conditions at the two stations continuously and compared the results.

BEN NEVIS AND BEYOND

In 1878, understanding of the way the Earth's atmosphere changed with height was sketchy. Ben Nevis was a candidate for a permanent meteorological observatory: it was the highest point in the British Isles, and its position on Scotland's west coast meant it stood square in the path of land-bound Atlantic storms.

What Alexander Buchan – secretary of the Scottish Meteorological Society – needed was someone to test the scientific case for an observatory. Someone who would make a sustained series of daily ascents to record the weather on a mountain, along the way experiencing and recording the most hazardous weather in the country. That person had to be obsessive, tenacious, stubborn and fit – not to mention capable of making delicate observations regardless of conditions. Whether Clement Wragge wrote to Buchan or Buchan to Wragge isn't entirely clear; but, either way, on 1 June 1881 Wragge the Mountain Meteorologist began a truly gruelling series of ascents up Britain's highest mountain.

In the summer of 1881, Wragge climbed Ben Nevis over 130 times. He would leave Fort William at 4.40am and reach the peak at 9am. His summit readings would be simultaneously matched by his wife Eleanora at sea level. He frequently reappeared in Fort William – with his companion, a Newfoundland Hound named Renzo – mid-afternoon dragging heavy clothes encased in frost. What Wragge found on the summit of Ben Nevis was an environment far more extreme than previously thought, articulated both in measurements and flamboyant prose.

Wragge's equipment was kept in a rude stone hut on the summit, which offered a brief and bitter respite. He frequently had to make a fire to thaw his numb fingers, and the final entry on 14 October describes the moment it went too far:

'The canvas roof of my hut has been carried away.
Winter has set in with extreme severity. I much regret
that observations must now be discontinued.'

A second year of observations saw Wragge gain an assistant to share the load. A *Times* reporter accompanied Wragge on one ascent, the pair crossing the summit – now nicknamed the Plateau of Storms – on all fours. The hysterical article gained considerable publicity, and in 1883 construction of a **permanently manned observatory** on the summit of Ben Nevis began.

Wragge was awarded the Gold Medal by the Scottish Meteorological Society for his reports, but did not win the role of observatory superintendent. By the time the observatory opened on 17 October 1883 Wragge was – possibly grumpily – on his way to Australia, complete with family, Renzo the dog and a cat.

RAGS, RICHES AND ROCKETS

In the three weeks following Wragge's arrival in Brisbane, an unprecedented 18 inches (457 millimetres) of rain fell – inspiring his excellent nickname 'The Inclement Rag'. Here, some of the more interesting observations about Wragge's character also emerged, which put his frequently acrimonious earlier life into context and painted a picture of a man who, while not exactly sociopathic, had something of a knack for falling out with people.

'He has a mop of flaming red hair, an explosive temper and the adjectival luxuriance of a bullocky' was the view of one contemporary in the Australian meteorological world, where Wragge quickly caused a stir by treading on many toes.

A windfall from a late aunt had made Wragge rich, so he set about building weather stations and founding observatories to further understand the Australian climate, and was soon working for the government. Many viewed this outspoken interloper with suspicion, and his methods spoke for themselves. Notoriously, he attempted to alleviate the Queensland droughts of 1902 by firing Steiger Vortex cannons at the sky above Charleville. These were supposed to burst rain from clouds, but Wragge wasn't there to see the experiment fail, having left town after an argument with the local council. But perhaps his most remarkable legacy was that Wragge began the tradition of naming storms after people. Tropical systems he named after South Sea Islanders he admired; cyclones after politicians he didn't.

Wragge became disillusioned with the Australian meteorological world – or possibly vice versa – in 1906, and

Between 1883 and 1904 The Ben Nevis Observatory, with a fire burning continuously inside, allowed observers to endure the most extreme conditions in the country to provide weather reports. This period of unbroken records was instrumental in modern weather forecasting: ball lightning, the aurora borealis and astonishing wind speeds (the Beaufort Scale had to be redrawn to allow for the extra velocity experienced) were all witnessed by a hardy band of observers who called this place home.

Wragge's incredible Steiger Vortex cannons, which were 18 feet (5.5m) long and shaped like 'conical candle snuffers'. The idea was to fire shells at clouds in order to create a vortex, which would release the rain.

decamped to New Zealand with an Anglo-Indian partner named Louisa Emmeline Horne. He established the Wragge Institute and Museum in Auckland, which would later be destroyed in a fire. Much of his time was spent lecturing on increasingly spiritual subjects, including his adopted faith of Theosophy. He also dabbled in the occult, partook in yoga and allegedly converted to Islam before his death in 1922 from a stroke. Pictured in later years, he resembled a gaunt mystic, in a garden like a jungle.

A footnote to Wragge's later years is found in a clipping from the *New Zealand Press* in 1916, which talks of Mr Clement Wragge, the 'astronomical lecturer', who gave a talk grandly entitled 'The Majesty of Creation'. The story is notable for an excellent accidental joke. 'The lecture was given in Mr Wragge's well-known breezy style,' it said. *SI*

'MAD' JACK CHURCHILL

The soldier who fought Hitler with bagpipes and a broadsword

As a cadet officer at Sandhurst in the mid-1920s, John Malcolm Thorpe Fleming Churchill managed to distinguish himself only in two ways: for smuggling a hot-water bottle into his bed (for which he was sternly reprimanded) and for turning up on parade with an umbrella. Challenged, he replied: 'Because it's raining, sir.'

Born in Sri Lanka in 1906 to a well-established Oxfordshire family, Churchill grew up loving history and poetry, had an encyclopedic knowledge of castles and trees, and felt a deep compassion for animals. After Sandhurst, he joined the Manchester Regiment and was sent to Burma. His sense of adventure first showed when he decided to drive his motorbike from Pune in the west of India to Burma – over 1,250 miles (2,000km) of dirt tracks and elephant trails – becoming the first person to cross the Subcontinent on two wheels, despite a near-fatal collision with an angry water buffalo.

When his regiment returned to Britain in 1936, Churchill soon got bored and left the army. He married a Scottish heiress and dabbled in a variety of jobs, editing a Kenyan newspaper, modelling for magazine adverts and playing cameo roles in films, including *The Thief of Bagdad* (1924) and *A Yank at Oxford* (1938). He mastered the bagpipes, entering a piping competition at the Aldershot Military Tattoo in 1938 as the only Englishman out of 70 entrants and causing a sensation by coming second. He also took up archery and was such a natural that in 1939 he represented Great Britain at the World Archery Championships in Oslo.

With the start of the Second World War, Churchill's life regained its purpose and he re-enlisted to fight the Germans. He had a theory that leaders in combat should act in a way that will simultaneously demoralize the enemy and convince his own men that nothing was impossible, so he led his men into battle playing the bagpipes and **brandishing a wooden longbow** and a claymore sword known as a claybeg. 'In my opinion, any officer who goes into action without his sword is improperly dressed,' he once said.

MARCH OF THE 'MAD' COMMANDO

On the retreat to Dunkirk, Churchill was wounded and carried a bullet in his shoulder for the rest of his life. Back in Blighty, he immediately volunteered to join a new military outfit called the Commandos. He didn't have a clue what a Commando was, but was keen because it 'sounded dangerous'. He was promoted to lieutenant-colonel and put in charge of No 2. Commando.

Their first mission was Operation Claymore – an amphibious raid on a German base in Norway. Churchill led his men ashore playing 'The March of the Cameron Men', and they blithely destroyed coastal defences, factories, radio transmitters, stores, a lighthouse, a power station, nine merchant ships and four Heinkels. They killed 150 Germans, captured 98 and brought 71 Norwegians back to the UK. The attack forced Hitler to deploy 30,000 extra troops to Norway, crucially weakening the southern part of his Atlantic defence.

Later, on a night raid in Italy, Churchill and a corporal crept from one German post to the next, capturing 42 prisoners at sword point. Churchill explained his secret:

Near the French village of L'Epinette, Churchill decided to ambush a German patrol and gave the signal to attack by silently taking down the German commander with an arrow. He was the last British soldier in history to have felled an enemy with a longbow.

121

'As long as you tell a German loudly and clearly what to do, if you are senior to him, he will cry "jawohl" and get on with it enthusiastically and efficiently, whatever the situation.'

Eventually, on an assault in Yugoslavia when every man under his command was killed or wounded and he had run out of ammunition, Churchill stood alone playing 'Will Ye No Come Back Again?' on his bagpipes until he was knocked unconscious by shrapnel and taken prisoner. They took him first to Berlin for interrogation in the mistaken belief that he was Winston Churchill's younger brother (also called Jack), then to Sachsenhausen Concentration Camp.

In September 1944, Churchill escaped Sachsenhausen but was recaptured and taken to a POW camp in Austria. He escaped again and marched 90 miles (145km) over the Alps until, limping and exhausted, he met up with some US soldiers in Verona and got back to England. By this time the war in Europe was over, so he went back to Burma, raring to fight the Japanese, but the Japanese surrendered before he had a chance. As Churchill ruefully told a friend: 'If it hadn't been for those damned Yanks, we could have kept the war going for another ten years.'

Undeterred, Churchill trained as a paratrooper, and on his 40th birthday he made his first parachute jump and flew straight to Palestine with a Scottish regiment. Now wearing a kilt and Glengarry bonnet to add to his claybeg, bagpipes and longbow, he was there to 'sort out' the war between the Jews and the Palestinians, risking his life on several occasions by walking straight into hostile gun range, grinning like a lunatic. 'People are less likely to shoot at you if you smile at them,' he explained.

After a spell training cadets in Australia, he settled for a desk job at the MOD but was still every bit an adventurer. He became the first daredevil to surf the Severn Bore; he collected 11 steam launches and sailed them on the Thames; he owned the fastest road-legal motorbike in the world; and he often alarmed fellow passengers on his daily commute by hurling his briefcase out of the train window. What they didn't know was that he was chucking it into his back garden to save him from having to carry it home. *RT*

ALFRED RUSSEL WALLACE

The unconventional evolutionist

Alfred Russel Wallace may now be recognized as having independently come up with the theory of natural selection at the same time as Darwin, but his remarkable contribution to science is not the main reason for his inclusion in this book. It is for his fearless spirit of enquiry and refusal to bow to establishment beliefs – even at the cost of personal hardship to himself and his family – that sets him apart. Wallace didn't just 'invent' evolution, he understood ecology before anyone else and, in his book *Island Life* (1880), anticipated the impact of invasive species, soil erosion and deforestation in degrading the environment. He was genuinely pioneering.

In another extraordinary book, *Man's Place in the Universe* (1903), he explored the likelihood of there being life on other planets in a way that could have been written yesterday. He took on astronomers who claimed there was water on Mars by explaining that the lack of atmosphere and gravity on the planet made it impossible for the 'canals' on Mars to actually be so. Some amateur!

Wallace didn't just observe the massive human and material waste that came from military adventures and write about it scornfully, he also recognized that the imbalance of power between the sexes was in a large part responsible for poor ecological thinking. Using his study of natural history, he became a firm champion for women's suffrage, writing extensively on the subject and putting himself at odds with most of his peers. He also railed against colonialism and the iniquity of contemporary land ownership, judging that any land unworked and unfruitful should be returned to the state. All of these views would have him seen as a left-of-centre leading thinker to this day.

Wallace was a brave man whereas his friend Charles Darwin was not. The former leapt into print with reckless frankness and no fear of consequences. Darwin, fearing social ostracism for his findings, dared to publish *On the Origin of Species* (1859) only after being pushed by Wallace's letter to him from Malaysia, in which he shared his insights on evolution and the role of natural selection.

For Darwin, this was the moment where he had to jump into print or see his life's work unrecognized. Without Wallace, one wonders what might have happened. Darwin would honourably co-publish his findings with Wallace and change the world of science for ever.

Wallace's background is now well known. From his early days in Wales, his failure as a developer and engineer, to his travels in the Amazon basin and the Malay Peninsula, which became the subject of a book, *The Malay Archipelago* (1869). It was an instant classic and remains in print to this day.

Wallace, like Darwin, had a passion for collecting; unlike Darwin, he did not have any great finances on which he could depend. He earned his money from selling duplicates from his collections and from his writing (the profits from which he consistently invested badly in mines, which went bust, or resources that no one eventually wanted). In a most unfortunate incident, he lost years of specimens in a shipwreck while returning from the Amazon.

Years later, Wallace was rescued from total poverty by his friend Darwin, who gathered a group of reluctant yet powerful voices in support. They awarded Wallace the Order of Merit and, with it, an annual income that would shelter him from the penury he faced.

His scientific reputation is now rightly emerging from under Darwin's shadow, but the interesting thing about him is not the acuity of observation that led to his scientific discoveries and having 'The Wallace Line' named after him as a result. It is the rigour of his intellect in applying the thought processes he brought to bear on the natural world to apply to the social governance of humankind. While the scientific principles of natural selection would be taken up by the Victorians as a judgement on the rightness of their established social order, Wallace riled against this in public, arguing for the fair distribution of useful land and for ownership to be time limited. It is extraordinary to see the principles he espoused coming to fruition as part of the legal framework for landholding in the People's Republic of China.

Wallace did, however, manage to antagonize almost every one of his scientific peers, by subjecting the topic of the afterlife and alternative lives to the same scrutiny as any other phenomena. He even had the temerity to give merit to some of the concepts, despite the proof that a number of famous clairvoyants and spiritualists had been fraudulent.

To be fair to Wallace, his was an exploding world of scientific revelation and these micro worlds were just being properly studied for the first time. Many scientists had an interest in spiritualism at the time. The mendacity of photography was not yet understood and one could well imagine Wallace being determined to find something of worth here. After all, he had done so elsewhere.

His dogged refusal to back down and toe the established line was quite remarkable – he became a laughing stock which probably caused the eclipse of his reputation for more than a century. But even here, there was something in his approach to thinking that demanded the removal of prejudice in a way that is totally admirable. Most of all, Wallace was an angry, ethical man, beautifully flawed and unconstrained by decorum. He was that most wonderful of human beings – a free spirit. *TS*

APSLEY CHERRY-GARRARD

The explorer who risked everything for a penguin's egg

Emperor penguins have a miserable life. They are confined to Antarctica, huddling together at the continent's edge. They incubate their eggs in the long Antarctic night, harassed by predators such as leopard seals and killer whales. These penguins are long-lived too, some of them enduring 50 years of grim existence. One of the great things about being human is not being an emperor penguin.

The cold, distant existence of these birds meant that little was known about their biology, and in 1910 it was thought they might hold a clue to one of the **great mysteries of evolutionary theory**. Investigating this was one aim of Captain Scott's Antarctic expedition, and it fell to three of his team to attempt a dangerous mission to the emperor penguin's breeding grounds, '...the weirdest bird's-nesting expedition that has ever been or will be'. These men were Henry ('Birdie') Bowers, Dr 'Bill' Wilson and Apsley Cherry-Garrard. Their journey turned out to be even less pleasant than being a penguin.

Cherry-Garrard was a rich young man, determined to give up his comfortable – and warm – life in England to join Scott's team. He was actually twice rejected by the expedition and, before his second application, made a significant donation. He didn't withdraw the money after rejection, and Scott was impressed enough to change his mind. The men travelled on *Terra Nova* in 1910, with the polar expedition planned for late 1911. The Antarctic winter was spent in preparation and scientific investigation, with Cherry-Garrard, Wilson and Bowers setting off in June to recover the eggs.

The journey was difficult from the start. Poor surfaces meant that the two sledges had to be moved separately, so that the group

The eggs were so highly prized because, at the time when *Terra Nova* set sail, biologists believed in recapitulation theory. This hypothesis – now discredited – suggests that developing embryos go through stages resembling their entire species' evolution during their gestation. Studying the Antarctic eggs would therefore show not only how emperor penguin species had evolved, but possibly how the entire family of birds had come to be.

walked three miles for every mile of progress. All this was carried out in the dark of the long Antarctic night, lit by candlelight or the moon. Their clothes would freeze solid, holding the men fixed in position. At nights they forced their way into frozen sleeping bags, which could take them an hour. Success was little reward, as they then had to rest in the damp beds. It took 19 awful days to complete the 67-mile (108km) trip and reach their destination. According to Cherry-Garrard, what followed was bliss compared to that first slog to reach the nesting grounds:

> '...Not because later our conditions were better – they were far worse – because we were callous. I for one had come to that point of suffering at which I did not really care if only I could die without much pain.'

Upon reaching their destination, they made an igloo only to be caught in a horrific blizzard. Their tent was blown away, condemning them to death if it could not be found before their return journey. To cap it all, the top of the igloo was blown away, too. The men could do nothing but lie in their sleeping bags, eating snow for moisture, waiting to die.

They spent two days there, sometimes singing hymns at the wind. It was so cold that Cherry's teeth shattered. He spent the time thinking back on his life and craving peaches with syrup. The men endured, never forgetting their pleases and thank yous. As Cherry-Garrard wrote, 'We kept our tempers, even with God.'

The explorers were saved by a 'one-in-a-million chance' – their tent had been carried by the wind only a short distance. Compared to the journey there the trip back was gruelling but easier, Cherry-Garrard repeating his mantra, 'You've got it in the neck, stick it, you've got it in the neck.' They returned with three eggs just in time to help with Scott's attempt to reach the South Pole.

While Cherry-Garrard did not join the five men on this final journey, he was part of the support team. Scott died with Wilson, Bowers and two others 12 miles (19km) from One-Ton Depot, defeated by blizzards, unseasonably cold weather and supply problems. Cherry-Garrard had been sent to wait at the depot, not knowing that the men were so close. It was unlikely that he could have saved the men anyway, and he'd been ordered not to proceed.

He returned, knowing the party was likely lost (although a later expedition of Shackleton's was saved by the supplies he left). A grim winter followed – the men of the expedition sleeping beside empty bunks, knowing that Scott was certainly dead.

'WE ALL HAVE OUR OWN WHITE SOUTH'

On his return to England, Cherry-Garrard took the three hard-won penguin's eggs to the Natural History Museum, where no one seemed interested. The scene was dramatized in his book as a discussion between the heroic explorer and a custodian, who doesn't

The response to Cherry-Garrard's clutch poignantly demonstrates how a paradigm shift in methodology can devalue data collected prior to the shift. During the four years that *Terra Nova* had been at sea, recapitulation theory had been largely discredited – which goes to show it really is ill-advised to put all of your eggs in one basket.

want the eggs ('This ain't an egg-shop'). Cherry-Garrard was **left in a corridor, waiting to be given a receipt**. When he visited the museum with Scott's sister some time later, the eggs could not be found. An ultimatum had to be made before they were located.

One of the eggs was put on public display for the first time in 2012, as part of the Natural History Museum's anniversary exhibition, 'Scott's Last Expedition'. In an interview with the *Guardian*, Douglas Russell, curator of the museum's 1.5 million eggs, said 'the ones that generate the most inquiries from the public – by a long way – are the three emperor penguin eggs

brought back from Scott's expedition. Some people want to check we still have the eggs, others want us to admit we have lost them.'

His time on the ice overshadowed much of Cherry-Garrard's later life. He wrote his account of the expedition, entitled *The Worst Journey in the World* (1922) – probably a better choice than his original title *To Hell: With Scott*. He returned at 27 and lived to 73, suffering from ongoing bouts of depression. He spent years re-calculating supplies, wondering if he might have saved Scott's team by disobeying orders. In Sara Wheeler's biography, she describes how his wife would encourage him to get out of bed, counting the steps he needed to make it to Regent's Park, an echo of his slow struggles on the ice.

Sometimes people go to extraordinary lengths and fail to achieve their goals. Scott's second expedition to Antarctica is famous for its lack of success. One of the greatest things to come out of that failure is Cherry-Garrard's book, *The Worst Journey in the World*. As gruelling as his journey was, his resilience is infinitely inspiring. As Shackleton tells us, 'We all have our own White South.' Cherry-Garrard never described his trials as wasted, writing: 'If you march your Winter Journeys you will have your reward, so long as all you want is a penguin's egg.' *JB*

NELLIE BLY

The journalist who flew into the cuckoo's nest

It's the winter of 1887, and in New York's municipal lunatic asylum on Blackwell Island a new inmate is being subjected to the humiliation and discomfort of an ice-cold bath.

> 'I began to protest. My teeth chattered and my limbs were goose flesh and bruised with cold. Suddenly I got ice cold water in my ears, nose and mouth. They dragged me out gasping, shivering and quaking, from the tub.'
> *–Ten Days in a Mad-house* (1887)

The young woman had been at the asylum only for a few days and found it to be one of the most unpleasant experiences of her life. Since the first night, she had been unable to sleep because of the hard bed and screams of other patients. She was appalled by the rancid food and frightened by the sadistic nature of many of the nurses and doctors. She witnessed patients bound together with rope and found some who appeared to be there for no other reason than their poverty or inability to speak English. Some of the women, she discovered to her horror, had been committed by cruel husbands wanting to be rid of them.

Like Randle McMurphy in *One Flew over the Cuckoo's Nest*, the woman was no ordinary inmate. She had faked her own insanity in order to get access to the asylum. Not for an easy ride, as McMurphy had foolishly hoped, but to investigate and expose the abuse of patients. For the fearless journalist Nellie Bly, this was the big scoop.

Bly was born Elizabeth Jane Cochran in 1864, in a wealthy Pennsylvanian family, and enjoyed writing from an early age. After moving to Pittsburgh in 1880, she read an article in her local paper *The Pittsburgh Dispatch* by a popular columnist, Erasmus Wilson. Wilson, a tiresome misogynist wrote that 'the working woman is a monstrosity' and went on to bloviate that women should not get 'fancy ideas about educating themselves'.

Cochran, choking back her morning cereal, wrote a brilliantly caustic response to the paper, signing herself 'Little Orphan Girl'. Impressed, the editor tracked her down and offered her a job. She took the pen-name 'Nellie Bly' (after a popular song of the day) and began to write her own column, exposing the poor working conditions for women in a local factory, and calling for reform of the country's divorce laws. Naturally, she ruffled a few feathers and before long found herself being relegated to cover the more 'feminine' topics of fashion and gardening.

Bly quit, relocated to New York and, after four tireless months of challenging the patriarchal institution of journalism, landed a job at the *New York World*. It came with a caveat. To prove her worth, the editor asked Bly for a report on Blackwell's lunatic asylum, housed on an island off Manhattan. No one anticipated her level of commitment to the article. Taking the name of a Cuban immigrant, Nellie Brown, she rented a room in a brownstone tenement and began to act insane. She claimed to hear voices, had conversations with ghosts and within a few days successfully acted her way into Blackwell's, fooling an array of doctors, specialists and a court judge. 'It is a human rat trap. Easy to get in, once in, it's impossible to get out,' she would later write in her book *Ten Days in a Mad-house* (1887).

After ten days Bly was released from Blackwell's when an agent from *New York World* came to collect her and prove (with some effort) that she was sane. Bly's exclusive exposé not only made her name, but instigated a full report on Blackwell's, leading to a million-dollar investment from the state and the promise that only the seriously mentally ill would be sent there in the future.

AROUND THE WORLD IN 72 DAYS

From here on in, Bly continued to delve into what her (jealous) fellow hacks named 'stunt' journalism. One week she was in a diving bell at the bottom of the ocean; the next she was undercover, exploring police corruption and the plight of unwanted babies. Then, in 1890, she persuaded the *New York World* to fund her on a round-the-world trip in an attempt to beat Phileas Fogg's fictional 80-day journey. As a single woman travelling alone, the journey would be an achievement in itself. Women were expected to take everything but the kitchen sink and half a dozen servants when travelling abroad; Bly simply packed two small bags and off she went.

During her 25,000-mile (4,000km) adventure she travelled by coach, train, rickshaw, horse, Chinese sampan and donkey. In France, she met author Jules Verne who saluted her heroic odyssey and gave her his favourite Breton shirt. She returned to America an even bigger hero. When Bly's name accompanied a newspaper headline, sales doubled.

Bly married Robert Seaman in 1894. She was 31; he was a 73-year-old millionaire running a company that made steel cans and barrels clad in iron. The company bore the imaginative name of Ironclad. Unsurprisingly, Seaman conked out a few years later and Bly took over the business. She worked hard to give the workers better rights and improve their working conditions, even building them a library for self-education. After an unfortunate case of fraud and embezzlement, however, Bly lost her husband's fortune. She left for Europe, intending to take a vacation but, still a journalist at heart, stayed there for five years as a First World War correspondent.

Of course, Bly wasn't going to do her reporting from behind a desk; she followed the action to the front line, risking life and limb for her features. She returned to New York in 1919 and continued to write and give lecture tours around America, until her death, aged 57.

Nellie Bly paved the way for investigative journalism as we know it today, never afraid to risk her life and reputation to help change the world for the better. If she'd been alive today, Bly would doubtless have fronted ground-breaking gritty TV documentaries, making Louis Theroux and Michael Moore's work look like a wet weekend in comparison. DB

MURIEL HOWORTH

The atomic gardener

Far away from the cares of Britain's Atomic Weapons Establishment, a pantomime cow was eating a radioactive lunch. A Geiger counter flashed and clicked as the cow stood up on her hind legs, rubbed her stomach and smiled. Moments later, a balletic Atom Man pirouetted, glided across the stage then squatted before Knowledge, a figure draped in parachute silk. 'The cow should soon be a perfectly healthy animal,' Knowledge said.

It's not clear if the ballet *Isotopia: An Exposition in Atomic Structure* was ever seen again after its debut in the Waldorf Hotel, in the heart of London's theatre district. Writing in October 1950, a *Time* magazine journalist recalled 13 members of the Ladies Atomic Energy Club gyrating across the stage in long evening gowns, as they danced and mimed the peaceful uses of the atom to a rapt crowd of 250 other women. *Isotopia* was one of many creations of the club's visionary founder, Muriel Howorth: script writer, choreographer, wardrobe advisor, poet, science-fiction novelist, former employee of the Ministry of Information and atomic evangelist. 'To lead women out of the kitchen and into the Atomic Age' was Howorth's aim. 'Not to know all about atomic energy and the wonderful things it can do is like living in the Dark Ages,' she wrote (*Atomic Gardening for the Layman* (1960).

Howorth wanted to take *Isotopia* to the Royal Albert Hall. She'd always been a fearless schemer, someone who knew how to marshal others' efforts. Despite having no formal science training, she taught herself the rudiments of nuclear physics at her home in the English seaside town of Eastbourne. By 1948, she'd set up her Ladies Atomic Energy Club and was already writing to the great physicists of the time, asking them to endorse her efforts. Einstein graciously sent some encouraging words.

As early as 1949, when she presented a model of a lithium atom to the surprised mayor of Eastbourne, Howorth was staging atomic stunts in public. There was a Sunday lunch that she ate in 1959, even though the potatoes and onions were three years old. They'd been stored in the labs of Harwell, Oxfordshire, with a few grains of radioactive sodium - enough to kill any germs (and all the taste).

In 1960, Howorth embarked on her most ambitious venture. Her intentions became public when she posed for the local papers, tickling an extraordinary plant that was growing on her windowsill. 'Yesterday I held in my hand the most sensational plant in Britain,' wrote Beverly Nichols, gardening correspondent for the *Sunday Dispatch*. 'To me it had all the romance of something from outer space. It is the first "atomic" peanut.'

This plant had itself been grown from a remarkable peanut – a gift from Oak Ridge Tennessee (home of the Manhattan Project). Like Howorth's onions and potatoes, this peanut had been irradiated. In this instance, all that atom blasting had done something extraordinary: it had disrupted the DNA of the peanut to create a mutant – a peanut that would grow into a giant plant, one with nuts as big as almonds. The plant itself wasn't radioactive – its crop tasted good and was perfectly safe to eat, just like any other peanut.

IN PRAISE OF THE MUTANT VEGETABLES

With food rationing in Britain still a recent memory, it's no wonder Howorth was drawn to the implications: take a large batch of seeds of wheat, barley, tomatoes or other foodcrop, irradiate them and, if you're lucky, you will make some mutants. Some of those mutants might grow in odd colours, some might grow tall or twisted, others will wither and die. But, if you're lucky, you may find that one-in-a-billion mutation: a plant that grows large enough to end world hunger. With her leadership, Howorth was sure the gardeners of Britain could work together to find this golden mutant.

Howorth instructed her husband, Major Howard, to set himself up as the sole European distributor of atom-blasted seeds from Van Hage Company in the Netherlands. She also persuaded Harold Wootton to exhibit her specimens in his Wonder Gardens, a pleasure garden in Wannock, a few miles outside Eastbourne. Thus her experimental, atom-blasted allotment was visited by thousands of families on Sunday afternoons on their way to the model village and tearooms.

Howorth opened the doors of her Atomic Gardening Society and asked for willing amateur gardeners to join her. This was citizen science on a grand scale, all handled through the Post Office. All you had to do was request some atom-blasted seeds from the Major and buy Howorth's book, *Atomic Gardening for the Layman* (1960), to jump into the atomic age.

Seeds were posted to volunteers, along with instructions on how to nurture them, log their growth and report back on any interesting mutants. Finding the golden mutant was a game of chance. Every volunteer and every new planting improved the odds of finding the plant that could, in Howorth's eyes, save humankind. The odds, however, were stacked against her. Howorth managed to recruit around 300 gardeners – but a thousand times that number would be needed to have any likelihood of creating even a handful of mutations, let alone the giant plant she longed for. To encourage the gardeners' competitive spirit, Howorth announced the most promising mutant each year would be awarded the 'Muriel Howorth Peanut Prize'. We don't know if anyone ever took home the trophy. Despite her optimism, by the mid-1960s, the volunteers had little to show for their efforts. The Atomic Gardening Society quietly fizzled out.

By this time, many plant scientists had abandoned atom-blasting, seeing it as a haphazard way to find useful mutants. They turned their attention to chemical methods of splicing the gene – techniques behind the GM crops of today. As atomic gardening historian Paige Johnson said to amusingplanet.com, 'If you think of genetic modification today as slicing the genome with a scalpel, in the 1960s they were hitting it with a hammer.' Howorth never reconciled herself to this, clinging to the romance of the atom until her death in 1971.

As an atomic pioneer, Howorth was a visionary. Although she never found her giant mutant, in many other ways, her work was a triumph. Decades before the era of crowd sourcing, she demonstrated that anyone could set up and run their own scientific experiments, following their own interests rather than the agenda of established laboratories. Long before anyone had ever spoken about open-source culture, she was already sharing scientific knowhow for the price of a few first-class stamps.

Howorth would be delighted to know that atomic gardening is making a comeback. In tightly controlled experiments, crop scientists are growing plants in circular fields that are continually bathed in radiation. This comes from highly radioactive cobalt-60 – a source so deadly, it has to be dropped into a lead-lined sarcophagus before anyone can enter the field. Rapid genome testing lets them sift through thousands of results. In *Atomic Gardening for the Layman*, Howorth hinted at plans for her own cobalt-60 garden, something she never had the funds to bring to fruition.

Howorth didn't have the chance to study atomic science formally, yet she came up with experiments that were rationally designed and breathtaking in their ambition. She achieved so much on that windowsill in Eastbourne, in Slaymaker's Wondergarden and in the pots of atomic gardening pioneers around the UK. Just think how much more she could have done if she'd been given the keys to the lab. SA

WILLIAM PRICE

The Welsh wizard

It's a cold winter's night in January 1884 and William Price, an 84-year-old Welsh druid sporting long flowing hair and a white robe, stands atop East Caerlan hill in South Wales. He places the lifeless body of his five-month-old son, Jesi Grist, into a parrafin-soaked casket and sets it alight. Villagers, leaving church that evening, see flames dancing on the hillside and are compelled to investigate. When they realize it is an act of blasphemy – the burning of a body – they transform into an angry mob. The child's half-charred corpse is snatched from the flames and Price is arrested and indicted. The news story will make the name William Price known across the Western world.

William Price was born in 1800 to a rural Welsh family. His father, the local reverend, suffered from mental illness and was taken to odd bouts of behaviour that included bathing fully clothed in ponds and stuffing his pockets with snakes. There was also a **wild streak in his son** who, in his teens shocked neighbours by running starkers across the local land, dancing and singing.

William Price was also exceptionally bright and became the apprentice of a local surgeon, before moving to London. Here, at the age of 21, he became the youngest ever member of the Royal College of Surgeons. While a brilliant career as a surgeon in the capital could have been his for the taking, Price turned his back on it; a profound love of Wales drew him back to the homeland.

After establishing himself as a highly respected surgeon in the Taff Valley, Price began to take an interest in druidism. Never one to do things by halves, he became the leader of a local order and shocked the community by declaring himself an atheist, naturist and vegetarian. Price also favoured a holistic

Price refused to wear socks and drank only champagne, but then he was his father's son, after all.

approach to his medical practice, believing that most diseases could be attributed to lifestyle. He was all too aware of how industrialization was affecting people's well-being, leaving them undernourished, dependent on prescription drugs and with polluted lungs. As such, he refused to treat smokers and recommended fresh air, exercise, healthy food and natural medicines to his patients.

Along with embracing his druidic roots, Price was becoming increasingly political. He helped set up a prototype national health scheme for local workers, established the country's first co-operative and fought to preserve the Welsh language and national identity. He also became a key local figure in the Chartist uprisings – a movement fighting for the rights of every man in the country to vote (rather than just a rich elite).

THE FULL PAGAN MAKE-OVER

Eventually, skirmishes between Chartists and the authorities led Price to flee for his life to France, dressed as a woman. Here, a mystical experience in the Louvre took him deeper into his pagan beliefs and, on his return, Price founded his own druidic order, grew his hair long and swapped conventional attire for red-and-green striped trousers and a gold waistcoat. For good measure, he plonked a fox skin on his head. He looked sensational.

At the ripe old age of 83, Price finally settled down and had a pagan wedding. His new wife, 60 years his junior, gave him a boy. Price named him Jesi Grist (Jesus Christ), announcing the child to be the new messiah for a pagan revival that would soon sweep through Britain. The boy died after only a few months, making Price a tragicomic figure in the eyes of many.

He chose to cremate the body – then an illegal act – leading to his arrest and a court case, which was reported across the world. Price, who always defended himself, put on his best pagan togs and gave an impassioned speech on the environmental impact of burials and the right of every person to be buried or cremated:

'It is not right that a carcass should be allowed to rot and decompose in this way. It results in a wastage of good land, pollution of the earth, water and air, and is a constant danger to all living creatures.'

Price was acquitted and the case paved the way for the Cremation Act of 1902. He sired another two children (including Jesi Grist the Second) and died at 93. Legend has it that his final words were: 'Give me champagne.'

While not everyone in Wales agreed with his beliefs and eccentricities, Price died a national hero. A few days after his death, atop the same windswept Welsh summit where Price had cremated his son, 20,000 people turned up for his cremation. Price, never one to miss a trick, had left instructions with his wife to ensure it was a ticketed event.

History remembers Price as a great philanthropist, druid and rebel who would have been heartened to see the resurgence of interest in neo-paganism in the West. His dress code, beliefs, vegetarianism and holistic approach to medicine would now make him a model citizen in such cities as Brighton, Portland, Berlin and Melbourne. In challenging convention and laws surrounding the disposal of the dead he was an early environmentalist and great catalyst for change.

When Price first attempted to cremate his five-month-old son in 1884, the story was widely reported in the press and attracted the attention of an aspiring writer. Being a medical man by trade, the story had particular resonance for him, and he penned a 3,000-word feature, based on the many accounts of the case he had collected. It was one of his first publications, printed in a Saturday journal called *For the Homes of the People*. The title of the fledgling writer's article, 'The Bloodstone Tragedy', gave an inkling of the literary work that would follow. Within a year, the young author would have his first real success with a detective story, 'A Study in Scarlet'. His name was Arthur Conan Doyle. DB

SEEKERS' DIRECTORY

FRANK BUCKLAND

BOOK G.H.O. Burgess, *The Curious World of Frank Buckland* (1967)

BOOK Frank Buckland, *Curious Men* (1880)

FIELD TRIP Head to Heston Blumenthal's The Fat Duck restaurant in Berkshire, to dine on snail porridge, crab ice cream and mock turtle soup and enjoy a modern zoophagy experience – thefatduck.co.uk

FIELD TRIP Visit the Scottish Fisheries Museum in Anstruther, Fife, where you'll find the Buckland Collection of fish casks – scotfishmuseum.org

CLEMENT WRAGGE

BOOK Simon Ingram, *Between the Sunset and the Sea* (2016)

BOOK Ken Crocket and Simon Richardson, *Ben Nevis, Britain's Highest Mountain* (2009)

BOOK William T Kilgour, *Twenty Years on Ben Nevis* (2014)

MAD JACK CHURCHILL

FILM You can catch a glimpse of Mad Jack in the 1952 film *Ivanhoe*, staring Elizabeth Taylor. He's one of the archers firing arrows from the walls of Warwick Castle.

APSLEY CHERRY-GARRARD

BOOK Sara Wheeler's *Terra Incognita: Travels in Antarctica* (1997), an account of her journey to Antarctica, features a journey to the remains of the Cherry-Garrard's igloo. Wheeler also wrote a biography of Cherry-Garrard, *Cherry* (2002), which includes the story of his later life and battles with depression

FILM Watch Werner Herzog's documentary *Encounters at the End of the World* (2009), which gives a sense of Antarctica's beauty and features a heartbreaking scene with a penguin.

FIELD TRIP Visit the Scott Polar Research Institute in Cambridge, where you'll find expedition artefacts from explorers' diaries to sleeping bags and sextants – spri.cam.ac.uk

FIELD TRIP Ask to see the penguin eggs in the Treasures Gallery at London's Natural History Museum.

BOOK Apsley Cherry Gerrard, *The Worst Journey in the World* (1922)

BOOK Herbert Ponting, *Eyewitness Accounts With Scott in the Antarctic* (2014)

NELLIE BLY

BOOK Read Bly's full account of her experience in the Blackwell's Island asylum (with sketches) in *Ten Days in a Madhouse* (1887).

BOARD GAME Follow in Bly's pioneering footsteps with a roll of the dice in this 1890 board game *Round the World with Nellie Bly*.

FIELD TRIP Visit the Nellie Bly Kaleidoscope Shop, which is the largest kaleidoscope in the world in Jerome, Arizona.

BOOK Nellie Bly, *Around the World in 72 Days and Other Writings* (1890)

ALFRED RUSSEL WALLACE

FIELD TRIP See Wallace's personal collection of insects, caught in South-east Asia 1854–62, at the Natural History Museum, nhm.ac.uk

BOOK Alfred Russel Wallace, *The Malay Archipelago* (1869, *left*)

DOCUMENTARY *Bill Bailey's Jungle Hero: Alfred Lord Wallace* (2013), two-part BBC documentary

MURIEL HOWORTH

GROW YOUR OWN Try your hand at growing 'atomically energized' plant varieties such as Tulip 'Faraday' (1949), Dahlia 'Ornamental Rays' (1966), Snapdragon 'Madame Butterfly' (1968).

TEDX TALK Sarah Angliss talks about the atomic gardening movement – bit.ly/OdditoriumMurielHoworth

DR WILLIAM PRICE

FIELD TRIP Visit the William Price statue and memorial gardens in Llantrisant, Wales.

BOOK Dean Powell, *Eccentric: The Life of Dr William Price* (2005)

4

PIONEERS & INVENTORS

4

PIONEERS & INVENTORS

In 2010, BBC Radio 4 ran an epic series called *A History of the World in 100 Objects*. Throughout the programme carefully chosen totems, paintings, figurines, pots and masks served as portals into the great empires and cultures of the past. However, the range of objects wasn't just restricted to art and craft. There were early stone chopping tools, astrolabes, credit cards and a solar-powered lamp – powerful reminders as to how our evolution is shaped by invention. We need only think of four of the greatest minds of the 19th century – Tesla, Edison, Bell, Morse – to remember what exponential leaps we have taken in the last hundred years through their work in telecommunication.

The sheer ambition of many pioneers and inventors is not, however, always tangible or demonstrable – particularly if their ideas failed to ignite during their lifetimes. Societal prejudices can also play a part in overshadowing great work – such as the vital contributions made to the discovery of DNA by Rosalind Franklin. She was overlooked in her day due to the fact that she was a woman.

Many individuals in this chapter had to contend with such problems during their lives. Madalyn Murray O'Hair dared to pioneer secularism in a deeply religious and patriarchal age; Flora Tristan wrote her own feminist version of *The Communist Manifesto* five years before Marx and Engels; and – against a tide of sexism and elitism – Elaine Morgan tirelessly campaigned to have a radical hypothesis on human evolution taken seriously, one which was eventually championed by Sir David Attenborough.

For sheer ambition over success we salute Paulo Soleri, who set out to build an entire city from scratch in the Arizona desert; Francis Galton, who attempted to measure the immeasurable (including boredom, beauty and the efficiency of prayer); and Buckminster Fuller, who devoted his life to inventing new forms of transport and housing, travelling the world umpteen times and pioneering global thought decades before the term 'global village' was coined.

On the flip side, it's worth remembering that some inventions only seem like a great idea at the time. Comedian Sid Caesar famously quipped: 'The guy who invented the first wheel was an idiot. The guy who invented the other three – he was a genius.' When it comes to Thomas Midgley Junior, who developed CFCs and leaded petrol for cars – this guy was not so much an idiot as a walking disaster zone.

FRANCIS GALTON

The man who measured the unmeasurable

In 1884, Francis Galton hit upon the idea of an 'attraction gauge' – a means of measuring, essentially, to what degree two people fancied each other. The idea effectively hinged on Galton's belief in a double meaning of the word 'inclination'. He reckoned that when someone felt an emotional inclination towards someone, they would also physically lean in towards them. Based on this premise, Galton imagined placing pressure pads under the chair legs of unsuspecting dinner party guests, then hooking these pads up to a pressure gauge to covertly monitor in a neighbouring room. The readings would then betray the diners' true feelings towards one another.

The attraction gauge is a classic example of Galton's thinking. He strove to take ineffable, abstract concepts and calibrate them; to take the emotional and the human, and to regulate it. In later life, Galton had his portrait painted. He wasn't that bothered about the artistic merit of the work. He was much more interested in the number of brush strokes taken to complete it, in the belief that there may have been an optimum number to produce the perfect painting. This was creativity, corralled by statistics.

The habit began at an early age. Galton was born in Birmingham in 1822, the youngest of seven children. Aged just 15, he enrolled as a medical student at Birmingham General Hospital. His introduction to the grisly world of Victorian medicine was uncompromising, as he accompanied doctors on their rounds and observed their operations. The teenage Galton theorized that he could identify the nature of the surgery an unfortunate and unseen patient was undergoing purely from their distinctive pattern of screams.

Galton was a true polymath, a seminal figure in subjects as weighty as heredity, statistical theory and meteorology.

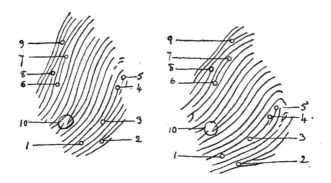

Galton developed fingerprinting as a forensic science, paving the way for its use in criminal cases. These prints (*right*) were used in the Scotland Yard account of a 1902 burglary.

Not only did he first observe the phenomenon of 'regression toward the mean' and develop the principle of 'the wisdom of the crowd' but, among many other achievements, he also discovered anti-cyclones and created the first newspaper weather map, coined the term 'eugenics', helped develop fingerprinting as a forensic science, and invented the dog whistle.

Galton's enquiries, as you might infer, weren't exclusively serious. In the 1840s, he spent months refining a formula designed to create the perfect cup of tea. By varying quantities and brewing time, he produced countless variations, making a note of the appeal of each. Having moved into a new marital home around the same time, he decided to find out, for absolutely no good reason, whether or not all the world's gold would fit in his house. It turned out it would all fit in his dining room with storage space to spare.

If this was relatively uncontentious, Galton's 1872 paper for the *Fortnightly Review*, 'Statistical Inquiries into the Efficacy of Prayer', was anything but. In this piece, he devised a statistical method that he claimed would prove whether or not praying worked. His premise is ingenious, if fairly preposterous. Galton argues that the health of sovereigns is routinely prayed for at church services. Therefore, kings and queens must be the most prayed-for people in their nation. It follows that, if praying works, royalty ought to have a greater life expectancy than members of other, comparable affluent groups. But Galton's research instead proved the opposite – that of all the affluent groups, including clergy and military officers, those involved in the fine arts and so on – members of royal households actually had the shortest life expectancy (excluding assassinations and other unnatural deaths). Prayer, he concluded, was therefore clearly an absolute waste of both time and kneeling.

Galton's paper provoked a predictably hostile response – although, entertainingly, it also obliged the religious establishment to undermine Galton's theory by arguing that generally, when members of the public prayed for the health of their sovereign, they probably didn't mean it.

DOCUMENTING WHAT IT MEANS TO BE HUMAN

Charting the seemingly undocumentable workings of the human mind was a challenge that Galton constantly relished. Differences in the way people visualized numbers and letters fascinated him, and led him to draw up elegant, if sometimes bewildering, diagrams of 'number forms', in which he effectively transcribed on to paper the mental landscape upon which his subjects described seeing consecutive numbers in their mind's eye. In *Inquiries into Human Faculty* (1883), he also recorded what would now be described as **synaesthetic connections between letters and colours**, including the lyrical and really quite lovely testimony of 'Mrs H, the married sister of a well-known man of science', who described the vowels thus:

'A, Pure white, and like china in texture.
E, Red, not transparent; vermilion, with china-white would represent it.
I, Light bright yellow; gamboge.
O, Black, but transparent; the colour of deep water seen through thick clear ice.
U, Purple.
Y, A dingier colour than I.'

Quite how trends in synaesthetic responses have changed since the mid-19th century is beyond the scope of this short biography, but it's a fair bet that if you asked people today what colour they associate with the letter 'I', the top five probably wouldn't feature 'gamboge'.

Colour also occupied Galton's thoughts when he wrote a letter to the journal *Nature* in 1879 titled 'The Average Flush of Excitement'. He recounted a trip to Epsom on Derby Day where, gazing at the main stand, he was afforded a view of the 'average tint of the complexion of the British upper classes'. Galton reported that the white 'sheet' of faces turned a uniform pink as the race reached its climax and excitement among the

Galton devoted many years to the study of 'composite portraiture' by combining the faces of subjects through repeated exposures. He was attempting to discover if there were any recognizable physiognomonic characteristics for health, disease or criminality. The results were ambiguous at best.

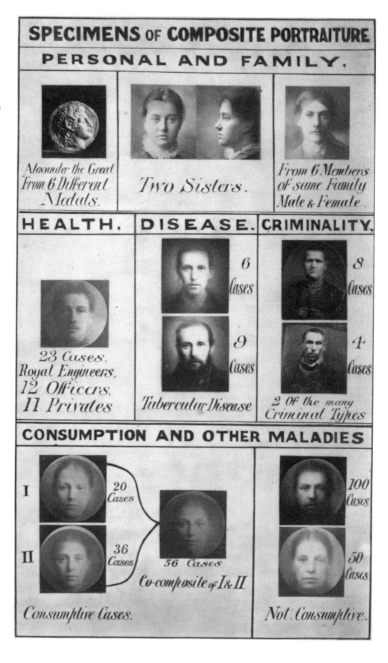

SPECIMENS OF COMPOSITE PORTRAITURE

PERSONAL AND FAMILY.

Alexander the Great From 6 Different Medals.

Two Sisters.

From 6 Members of same Family Male & Female.

HEALTH. DISEASE. CRIMINALITY,

23 Cases. Royal Engineers. 12 Officers. 11 Privates

6 Cases

9 Cases

Tubercular Disease

8 Cases

4 Cases

2 Of the many Criminal Types

CONSUMPTION AND OTHER MALADIES

I

II

20 Cases

36 Cases

56 Cases
Co-composite of I & II

Consumptive Cases.

100 Cases

50 Cases

Not Consumptive.

punters correspondingly peaked. On this occasion, he offered no formula for correlating average skin tone and mood, but you can be pretty sure the idea crossed his mind.

By the mid-1880s, Galton's attempts to measure the immeasurable had stepped up a gear. The paper 'Measure of Fidget', published in *Nature* in 1885, proposed a 'boredom index'. Galton had noticed, while attending lectures, that the more rapt the audience, the straighter they would sit in their seats. Consequently, if engaged by the lecture, the distance between their heads would be roughly equidistant. If, on the other hand, the presentation was a bore, the audience would begin to slouch and slump, thereby rendering the distance between their heads more irregular. The more even the spacing, therefore, the more interesting the talk. It was a typical Galton statistical correlation – one which, equally typically, he was unable to render into an applicable formula. 'I endeavoured to give numerical expression to this variability of distance,' he confessed , 'but for the present have failed.'

In 1888, Galton's counting obsession reached, perhaps, its apotheosis. What was meant to be a relaxing holiday in Vichy with his wife Louisa was instead dominated by Galton's covert attempts to record the amount of time taken by various passers-by to walk between two fixed points on the street, followed by the similarly clandestine categorization of local women into six size categories, from 'thin' to 'prize fat'.

In the same year, Galton travelled from city to city, surreptitiously counting the number of beautiful, average-looking and ugly women, before returning to London and collating the results into a 'Beauty Map of Great Britain'. Sadly, there seems to be no extant completed map, although we know that at either end of the beauty scale, according to Galton, lay London and Aberdeen. Readers may speculate which came top and which, according to Galton, had been hit with the city-wide ugly stick.

Galton died in 1911, after a period of illness. His last words were believed to be, 'One must learn to suffer and not complain.' But even then, you suspect, the scientist's fading mind was probably preoccupied with how one might best go about calculating the statistical correlation between suffering and complaint. DM

FLORA TRISTAN

The woman who defied society

Though he never met her, the painter Paul Gauguin had much to say about his grandmother. 'She was an astonishing woman,' he wrote in 1903, 'a bluestocking, socialist, anarchist and credited with having founded the trade union movement.
She was probably a terrible cook.' (Charles Neilson Gattey, *Gauguin's Extraordinary Grandmother* (1970)).

While it's hard to gauge the sentiment behind the last sentence, Gauguin was right on every other count. His grandmother Flora Tristan was a woman who experienced great injustices and cruelty at the hands of society and responded by challenging them head on. A true pioneer, she was arguably the first to see the parallels between women and workers – advocating an alliance between society's two most oppressed groups that would transcend boundaries and be strong enough to take on the established order, the government and even the church. Despite publishing her essay *The Workers' Union* (1843) five years before Marx and Engels wrote *The Communist Manifesto* (1848), Tristan's life and works are almost entirely overlooked. She doesn't even make it into the Wikipedia entries on the history of feminism or socialism.

TRAVELS OF A SOCIAL PARIAH
Tristan's early life was marked with such turbulence, it could have been penned by Dickens. She was born of mixed heritage in Paris at the turn of the 19th century – her mother was French, her father an exiled Peruvian aristocrat from one of the country's most powerful families. He died when she was only four but, as Tristan was considered illegitimate under French laws, neither mother nor daughter were permitted to inherit his estate. Tristan

grew up in abject poverty. To escape destitution, at 17 she married her boss André Chazal, an engraver who owned a workshop in Montmartre. The pair were ill-matched and the relationship soon grew violent.

Though badly treated, Tristan was legally unable to divorce her husband. Already a strong-willed woman, she yearned to be free of him, later writing: 'True, he's a despicable creature… you cannot escape his yoke! Feel the weight of the chain which makes you his slave and see if… you can break it!' (*Peregrinations of a Pariah* (1838)). Pregnant with their third child, the 21-year-old Tristan did something unthinkable in 19th-century Paris – she packed her bags and walked out on him.

After a solo trip to Peru, in which she unsuccessfully attempted to claim her paternal inheritance, Tristan headed to England for the first of four trips. Here **she mixed with all levels of society** – dropping in on fashionable literary circles, meeting gypsies, prisoners and prostitutes, and documenting the full impact of industrialism in England in her 1840 book *Promenades in London*. Throughout her journals in these years, she shows herself to be an acute observer with an insatiable thirst for knowledge.

Tristan even managed to smuggle herself into the Houses of Parliament wearing the clothing of a Turkish diplomat.

If Tristan thought her husband's temper would have cooled by the time she returned to France, she was wrong. Chazal pulled a gun on his wife and left a bullet lodged in her chest. With attempted murder deemed suitable grounds for divorce, Tristan was finally able to free herself of her marital 'chain', although not the judgement of her peers.

Rather than shrink away, Tristan decided to face society head on. Throwing herself passionately into the emerging politics of socialism and women's rights, she began to lecture and write. Her next book, *The Peregrinations of a Pariah* (1838), is a candid autobiographical account of how she was perceived as a 'little tramp' in both Peru and France. However, the culmination of her politics and utopianism came in what followed – the world's first revolutionary feminist-socialist handbook, *The Workers' Union* (1843). A pioneering blend of socialism and feminism, it begins:

'Workers, your condition in present society is miserable and painful: in good health, you do not have the right to work;

sick, ailing, injured, old, you do not even have the right to care; poor, lacking everything, you are not entitled to benefits…
The fate of the animal ruminating in a stable is a thousand times better than yours. He, at least, is certain of eating the next day.'

Within the essay, Tristan lays out her vision for a 'Worker's Union Palace' – a co-operative that would offer housing, factories, hospitals and education. It would be a safe house providing better education for all, created and paid for by the workers who would each put in a small amount of money.

'WORKERS, WITHOUT WOMEN, YOU ARE NOTHING!'

In mixing socialism, feminism and activism, Tristan was forging an unchartered path. She became one of the first to see parallels between the problems facing workers – survival, education and sense of self – with that of women. She not only saw strength in an alliance between these two oppressed groups, but even proposed that the workers' emancipation was not possible without female liberation.

Tristan was one of the first to document the significance of an emerging class of earners, and to attempt to share this knowledge with workers in order to bring about their liberation – speaking directly to the working class rather than to the enlightened middle classes. She even foresaw the inevitable danger of class hostility, but hoped to show the propertied classes that it was in their interests to help the progress of the workers.

As Marx and Engels would do in *The Communist Manifesto* (1848), Tristan was calling for a systematic union of workers. In adding women's rights into the equation, her manifesto was, arguably, more far-reaching and radical. Unlike Marx and Engels, she had direct experience of poverty and social inequality. She didn't have a ridiculous beard either.

THE JOURNEYWOMAN

Her trip also echoed the Russian Populists, who travelled from peasant village to village educating the masses about their situation.

In the final year of her life, Tristan embarked on a gruelling tour of industrial France to lecture workers and help communities establish her Union Palaces. She **followed old journeyman's trails**, travelling solo by stagecoach or river boat, visiting workshops, dropping in on churches and factory owners, and tirelessly writing letters to reach out to grassroots organizations. Her journals document her advancing illness (most likely typhoid), along with her despair as she was repeatedly rejected by the workers, together with moments of joy and genuine connection.

Tristan died during her tour, aged 41. Her funeral was attended by people from all walks of life – writers, carpenters, lawyers, journalists, blacksmiths, townswomen and over 100 workers, who took turns carrying the casket, which weighed almost nothing.

Flora Tristan was a true outsider who dedicated her life to preaching unity. Her personal struggles were tough and numerous – for the right to inherit, the right to divorce an abusive husband and the right to have custody of her children – but none was unusual for women at the time. What makes Tristan a true radical was that, when faced with such suffering at the hands of men, poverty and politics, she fought back with every stitch of her being – not just for herself, but for the salvation of our entire society.

A unfaltering pioneer, she remains one of the most overlooked feminists and utopian socialists in history. But why she is so overlooked is still unclear. Perhaps she was overshadowed by Marx and Engels, who followed so closely after her. Perhaps, we just weren't ready for such radical viewpoints. Either way, it's about time we rediscover this wholehearted, naive, unblinkingly frank and fearless thinker. DB

ELAINE MORGAN

The housewife who championed the aquatic ape theory

Ever wondered why men grow beards and women don't? Why newborn babies can instinctively swim and hold their breath under water? Why, unlike most mammals, our noses are hooded?

In 1930, a marine biologist named Alister Hardy came up with an alternative theory of human evolution. He proposed that our ancestors didn't just come down from the trees and begin running around on two legs, lobbing spears about. Instead, he proposed that, for a time, we had a semi-aquatic existence, which led to many of the unique features that differentiate us from primates.

Hardy's hypothesis was triggered by a realization that humans have a layer of subcutaneous fat, which is unique to land animals and akin to the blubber of aquatic mammals. He suggested that a rise in sea levels led our ancestors to lagoons, seashores and other watery habitats for a considerable period, where we took to wading and swimming. Hardy speculated that our nakedness, bipedalism and streamlined bodies were a result of long-term adaptation to water, not from wandering the plains of Africa as the more established 'Savannah theory' proposed. Fearing that the controversy of such a idea would compromise his academic career, Hardy kept the hypothesis a secret for 30 years. When he did come to write about it in 1960, it was duly dismissed by his peers.

Time to introduce our heroine, Elaine Morgan. In the 1960s, Morgan was establishing herself as a fearless and witty writer with a sharp intellect and fascination for evolutionary theories. When she came across Hardy's thesis, his ideas rang true. As a feminist, she held a deep frustration that all prior established theories of human evolution were inherently sexist. Morgan recognized that evolutionists had, for too long, considered human adaptation only from a male perspective.

> 'I rejected this idea of the male as a mighty hunter and weapon wielder and female as mere child-bearer.'
> –Elaine Morgan, *The Descent of Woman* (1972)

In questioning the notion that humans lost their hair to avoid overheating when chasing prey in the plains, she pointed out:

> 'Unfortunately for the Tarzanists, it was the stay at home female who became nakedest, and the over-heated hunter who kept the hair on his chest.'

Morgan decided to write a book that would look at human evolution from a female perspective, while simultaneously exploring Hardy's aquatic ape theory. *The Descent of Woman* (1972) was a sensation. In it, Morgan single-handedly takes on Sigmund Freud, *The Naked Ape* author Desmond Morris, Charles Darwin and God (via Genesis). All of them, Morgan argues attempted to explain the world from a male-centred perspective:

> 'Throughout most of the literature dealing with the sexes, there runs a subtle underlying assumption that woman is a man gone wonky. The deeply rooted semantic confusion between man as a male and man as a species has been fed back into and vitiated a great deal of the speculation that goes on about the origins, development and nature of the human race.'

THE DESCENT OF WOMAN

The Descent of Woman was eventually translated into 25 languages, offering Morgan the opportunity to travel the world, appear on talk shows and take part in live debates. She was often introduced as 'a housewife from Wales'.

The academic reaction to Morgan's book was largely hostile. *The Descent of Woman* and the aquatic ape hypothesis in general were snubbed as pseudoscience. Anthropologists pointed out that the arguments were mere speculation and not based on testable scientific theory. Morgan was written off for being a mere journalist and, by some, as a woman with an axe to grind.

Over the decades that followed, Morgan never faltered in her support for and research into the aquatic ape hypothesis, publishing more books – *The Aquatic Ape* (1982), *The Scars of Evolution* (1990) and *The Naked Darwinist* (2008) – and becoming more rigorous with her scientific research. In exploring water births she found the experience was perceived as more natural, comfortable and relaxed by the majority of midwives and mothers. She discovered that human babies are born with a diving reflex to close the throat when immersed in water, that our heartbeats slow down when we enter water, and that swimming is one of the safest and best all-round forms of exercise for mind and body. For Morgan, and many others, the aquatic ape hypothesis just made sense: 'If it is sound it will prevail anyway, if it is not sound, it doesn't deserve to' (TED, 2009).

Morgan kept flying the flag for aquatic apes, giving a TED Talk in 2009 at the age of 85 and still clearly irritated that the hypothesis hadn't been fully investigated by science. 'The aquatic ape hypothesis has long been dismissed with the yetis and the Loch Ness monster,' she complains.

While the Savannah theory has since lost favour (with little to replace it), a trawl through the Internet will quickly reveal the degree of hostility that remains towards Morgan and Hardy's hypothesis. In a surprise move, however, a few years before Morgan's death, Sir David Attenborough came out to support the theory. He even made a two-part BBC documentary to challenge criticisms that there was nothing testable about the hypothesis.

One aspect of the theory focuses on the layer of waterproof grease found on newborn human infants, known as *vernix caseosa* (literal translation: cheesy varnish), not known to occur in any other primates. If there was credence in the aquatic ape hypothesis, Attenborough reasoned, other semi-aquatic mammals should have it too. The theory held out: *vernix caseosa* was discovered to be present on newborn harbour seals as a means of dealing with the cold; the thicker the coating is, the quicker the pups can take to the water.

The scientific world seems to remain critical of the aquatic ape theory, despite recent advances and the fact that other theories appear equally untestable. And while it seems unlikely that Hardy's theory can neatly explain our transformation from tree-dweller to trouser-wearer, it may at least prove to be a key element in a more complex evolutionary history of humankind. If (or when) it does, this 'housewife from Wales' may prove to be one of the great unsung heroes of modern science. DB

ARGUMENTS FOR AND AGAINST THE AQUATIC APE THEORY

For:

1 **Nakedness.** Most mammals that have lost their body hair have been conditioned by water, for example dugong, walrus, dolphin, hippopotamus. The majority of land mammals have hair.

2 **Bipedality.** All apes and monkeys are capable of walking on two legs. The only time they always walk on two legs is when wading in water.

3 **Fat.** Humans have a fat layer outside the body wall inside the skin, known as subcutaneous fat, or blubber. Unlike land mammals, infants are born with plenty of fat for the first 12 months, providing insulation and buoyancy.

4 **Natural intimacy with water.** Infants instinctively know how to hold their breath and swim under water.

5 **Hair.** Hair follows the flow of water, providing something for babies to hold on to. Beards easily distinguish men when only heads are seen bobbing in water.

6 **Speech.** The only mammal to ever copy the sounds of human speech was Hoover, a domesticated harbour seal, who learned to mimic the voices of the couple who rescued him and raised him in their bath.

7 **Nose.** A hooded nose prevents water from easily entering the nostrils. The only other example of this on a primate is in the (aquatic) proboscis monkey.

8 **Brain size.** The brains of Savannah animals shrunk over time while human brains grew threefold. To evolve a larger brain humans needed an abundant supply of omega 3. The only place to find this would have been the shoreline.

Against:

1 **Most primates don't like water.** The exception being the proboscis monkey.

2 **No fossil evidence as yet exists.** Despite the long time period needed for these developments to take place, there is no fossil record.

3 **Predators.** Crocodiles and sharks would have found humans easy prey.

4 **Fur.** Some aquatic mammals do have fur, for example otters, beavers.

5 **Testicles.** Aquatic mammals have internal testicles to insulate them.

6 **Water births.** If babies were born in sea water, they would get cold too quickly and die.

4:04

BUCKMINSTER FULLER

The Dymaxion man

It's 1920 and a broken man stands on the edge of Lake Michigan. Bankruptcy, the death of his daughter, an affair with a teenage girl and a drink problem have led him to this point. As he prepares to cast himself into the dark waters, a nagging thought occurs to him: does he have the right to take his own life? After all, he reasons, his life doesn't just belong to him, it belongs to the whole of humanity. Eschewing the devil he makes a pact with humankind – from this day on he will dedicate his life to the betterment of the whole planet. The man's name is Buckminster Fuller.

To understand Fuller's legacy, we must pause and contemplate the name of a Scottish Indie band, We Were Promised Jet Packs. Back in the early part of the 20th century, many fostered a spirit of optimism for a leisure-rich future, where domestic chores would be carried out by subservient robots and everyone would drive bullet-shaped cars and whizz through the skies propelled by rocket belts.

Technology, we believed, would be our saviour and liberator. But after the inhumanity of the world wars, when machines were used for mass slaughter and destruction, such utopianism was replaced by a more pragmatic vision of the future. While the promise of jet packs remains unrealized, no one in the 20th century was more committed to fulfilling the Jetsons' lifestyle than Buckminster Fuller – not just for America but the whole of humanity.

After his epiphany by Lake Michigan, Fuller (or 'Bucky', as many knew him) threw himself head first into life. His new motto was: 'I look for what needs to be done. After all, that's how the

universe designs itself.' He could see that the planet had more than enough resources to eliminate poverty, housing shortages, transport problems and pollution. Our only problem was that we didn't think globally. **He coined the phrase 'spaceship earth'** and reasoned:

> 'The planet is essentially a giant spaceship, with no instruction manual, that governments and corporations are all trying to steer it in different directions. They forget that, really, we live in a one town world.'
> – Buckminster Fuller, *Operating Manual for Spaceship Earth* (1968)

Decades before environmentalism became a movement, Fuller was promoting his own concept of a global village.

DYMAXION BY DESIGN

Everything Fuller invented was driven by a principle he called Dymaxion – a portmanteau of the words dynamic, maximum and tension. Rather than relying on compression (such as the weight of bricks for housing), he saw tension as a means of providing the greatest efficiency through available technology.

Viewing American cars as inefficient, heavy, noisy and unstreamlined, he invented the Dymaxion car, which was five times more efficient in miles to the gallon and boasted top speeds of 110 miles per hour (177km/h). It was also bullet-shaped, 6 meters (20ft) long, three-wheeled, carried up to 11 passengers and based on aviation technology.

One unexpected side-effect of Bucky's vehicle was that its 'wow' factor could bring whole roads to a standstill. After its arrival in New York created a seven-hour gridlock, Fuller was politely asked never to drive it through the city again.

Fuller came tantalizingly close to having his Dymaxion car mass-produced but, being tubular, it was easy to overturn and, after a test-drive resulted in a fatal accident, investors backed off. Undeterred, he **turned his attention to America's housing crisis and formulated the Dymaxion house** – built with the same efficiency of engineering he saw applied to suspension bridges.

The house, which resembled a UFO, was suspended on a mast and built from aluminium and plastic with a revolving roof. Weighing only one-fiftieth of a typical American house, it was tornado-proof and self-cleaning and could be disassembled and transported by lorry. The interior, with its dust-proof hat rack and conveyor-belt linen closet, was every bit the house of the future.

In order to get everything done, Buckminster Fuller even created his own Dymaxion sleeping pattern, whereby he napped for 30 minutes every six hours. In a 1943 interview with *Time* magazine, he admitted to finally dropping the schedule as it 'conflicted with that of his business associates, who insisted on sleeping like other men'.

Again, Bucky came achingly close to seeing mass production of his idea before investment dried up. However, his Dymaxion house paved the way for his best-known work – **the geodesic dome** – a semicircular structure designed with sophisticated geometry and using the Dymaxion principle of tension. Such a building could be pieced together in seven hours to create a weather-proof structure resembling a giant igloo.

Fuller lived in a geodesic dome with his wife for 12 years and constructed a giant one for the 1967 Montreal World's Fair, which still looks out of this world. Ever the visionary, he designed domes for underwater farms, floating cities and geodesic churches. He even proposed using **giant domes to shield cities from hostile weather**.

Over 100,000 geodesic domes exist around the world – two of the most celebrated being the adjoined biomes at the UK's Eden Project and an almost fully spherical Spaceship Earth at the Epcot Center in the United States. Fifty years on, they still look futuristic.

The structure for the geodesic dome was actually the work of German inventor Walther Bauersfeld, who designed it for a planetarium. Fuller popularized the design and gave it its name.

An idea that was employed inversely in *The Simpsons Movie* (2007) to protect the outside world from a nuclear leak at Springfield, caused by Homer, a mutant squirrel and a pet named Spider Pig.

OPTIMISTIC TO THE END

A short man with bottle glasses, Fuller was an unlikely candidate as a ladies' man but his infectious enthusiasm and ability to talk ten to the dozen certainly gave him charisma. He transcribed his ideas into 28 books and travelled the world over 120 times, delivering **epic lectures that could last up to 12 hours**.

With a growing determination to challenge the self-serving attitudes of corporations and politicians, by the 1960s Fuller had created a Dymaxion game that included a map of the world's resources. He wanted to show world leaders and CEOs that the earth had enough land and materials to take care of everyone, if only we worked collectively. Decades before the Internet and social media, Fuller was thinking like a network.

Fuller died in 1983 aged 87, still lecturing and never losing his belief that 'it would all work out'. Technology may have moved on since his pioneering designs but his philosophy is still relevant. If more of us had the courage to think like Fuller, our future may still be one in which we eliminate poverty, provide Space Age housing for all and whizz around on jet packs. Environmentally friendly ones, of course. DB

Bucky's words had the ability to confuse, inspire and exhaust audiences. In exploring his lectures online, a strong caffeine fix beforehand may be required, but you will be richly rewarded nonetheless.

JOHN HUNTER

The surgeon who stole an Irish giant

This is the story of two men: Scotsman John Hunter, surgeon to the king, and Irishman Charles Byrne, circus attraction. Two men from very different worlds whose paths crossed in 1783 in London. Byrne, who spent his last years in terror of his body falling into the hands of anatomists, and Hunter, who was determined to be the man to dissect the Irish giant.

In 1761, Charles Byrne was born near Lough Neagh in Ireland, to parents of average height and modest means. Here he grew up, and up and up, until he had reached a height that marked him as a giant and a 'freak'. Over 8 feet (2.7m) tall, according to contemporary accounts. Modern science, ever the party pooper, says it was closer to 7 feet 7 inches (2.3m).

At the age of 19, Charles Byrne left home and began a journey that would see him become famous enough to be mentioned by Charles Dickens in *David Copperfield* and later used as a character in Hilary Mantel's 1998 novel *The Giant, O'Brien*.

Byrne started by touring Scotland and the north of England, promoting himself as an attraction, and charging the curious 2s 6d (about 12.5p) to stand and gawp at him. By the time he reached London in 1782, his fame had spread and he became, quite literally, a short-lived phenomenon.

Byrne's base of operations in London was Cox's Museum in Charing Cross, an establishment set up to display unusual exhibits – Oliver Cromwell's head was another popular attraction. Byrne lived in an apartment next door, furnished with cane furniture specially made for his gargantuan dimensions.

Byrne, however, was not coping well with the pressures of fame. It's hard to imagine what his day-to-day existence must have been like. A person of his size, a man who could light his pipe from the gas lamps that lined the streets, could never be offstage, never blend into the crowd or cease to be the object of startled attention. On top of this, he woke from one particular night of drunken revelry to find that his life savings had been stolen from his pocket. The Irish giant, already suffering from tuberculosis and alcoholism, went into a steep decline.

Above all, he had one overriding fear. Anatomists circled Byrne like sharks smelling blood. It wasn't until 1832 that prohibitions concerning the use of cadavers in medical research would be eased. These strict laws had caused such a demand for black-market corpses that murder was on occasion committed simply because of the victim's resale value. In this climate, where corpses of an average size were keenly sought, Byrne's body would have been highly valued. It wasn't that he feared being killed for his body, at least according to newspaper reports of the time; it was a morbid terror of post-mortem dissection. Byrne was the research opportunity of a lifetime, and he knew it.

THE GIANT'S FINAL WISH
Byrne made special arrangements in the event of his death. He was to be buried at sea, so that no scientist with a shovel, a winch and a surfeit of enthusiasm could dig him up. And his coffin was to be lead-lined, just to make sure it was a tough nut to crack. He paid friends and some fishermen to ensure his wishes were respected, reiterated his burial conditions in the strongest possible terms on his deathbed, and died in June 1783 at the age of 22.

This is the point at which John Hunter enters our story. Hunter was a distinguished and accomplished fellow indeed. A Scottish surgeon and early proponent of the scientific method, he can justifiably claim credit for improving our understanding of inflammation, gunshot wounds, venereal diseases – he once infected himself with gonorrhoea and syphilis for his research – child development and most pertinently, bone growth.

Having started out assisting with dissections for his elder brother William and his brother's former tutor, the fabulously named William Smellie, Hunter had risen to stratospheric heights in the medical profession. He became a Fellow of the Royal Society in 1767, surgeon to St George's Hospital in 1768, and

A 1794 etching showing Charles Byrne (*the tall fellow, centre*), a dwarf named George Cranstoun and three average-sized men.

Byrne, Cranstoun & others

P. 909.

personal surgeon to King George III in 1776. In short, this was a man whose wishes were to be respected. Even if those wishes involved dissecting the corpse of a recently deceased Irish giant who had made meticulous provisions to avoid that eventuality.

A BONE OF CONTENTION

Reports on how much Hunter paid to have Byrne's body removed from its coffin range from £130 to £500, which would be around £35,000 today. Whatever the amount, the bribe was accepted, Byrne's coffin went to the bottom of the sea filled with rocks, and John Hunter spirited the giant's remains away. He chopped the body into pieces, boiled away the flesh and kept very quiet about the huge skeleton in the back room.

In fact, it was four years before Hunter conceded that he was in possession of Charles Byrne's bones. Was the subterfuge justified? In 1909, an examination of the skeleton revealed that Byrne had a pituitary tumour, and in 2011 researchers discovered that the giant had a rare gene mutation involved in such tumours. The skeleton has also proved vital in helping to link acromegaly, the overproduction of growth hormone, to the pituitary gland.

John Hunter was a difficult, brilliant man, described by a contemporary as 'warm and impatient, readily provoked, and when irritated, not easily soothed'. The Hunterian Society of London was later named in his honour, and the Hunterian Museum, at the Royal College of Surgeons in London, houses his collection of anatomical specimens, including the skeleton of Charles Byrne.

This is where it will stay, for now – despite ongoing pressure for the body to be buried. Dr Sam Alberti, current director of the Hunterian Museum, says: 'The Royal College of Surgeons believes that the value of Charles Byrne's remains, to living and future communities, currently outweighs the benefits of carrying out Byrne's apparent request to dispose of his remains at sea.' *MB*

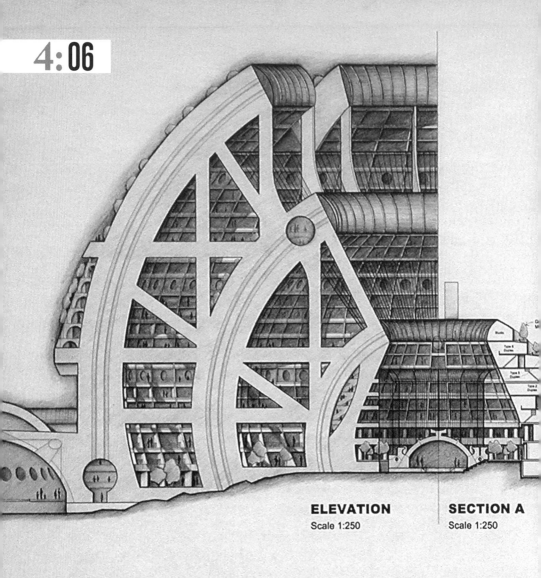

4:06

ELEVATION
Scale 1:250

SECTION A
Scale 1:250

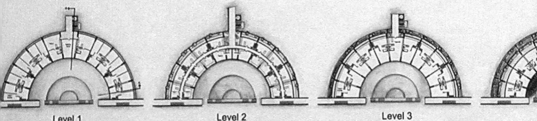

Level 1   Level 2   Level 3

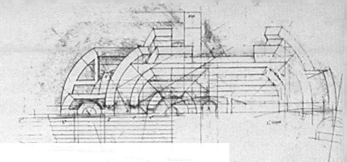

PAOLO SOLERI

The man who built a city in the Arizona desert

In the late 1960s, Italian architect Paolo Soleri began a monumental experiment 70 miles (113km) from Phoenix in the Arizona desert. Perceiving an 'epidemic of suburban sprawl in modern cities' (*The Urban Ideal* (2001)), Soleri decided to show the world how a super-city should look, by building his own from scratch.

Soleri came to Arizona as a disciple of Frank Lloyd Wright, a visionary American architect who designed organic structures that harmonized with their environments. After a few years back in Italy practising ceramic making and bronze casting (skills that would soon prove to be essential), Soleri returned to the States to embark on his life's work.

He snapped up 4,000 acres (1,620ha) of Arizona desert and revealed his great vision: Arcosanti, a low-impact monolithic eco city that would foster human interaction through architecture. Occupying 25 acres (10ha), this epic single structure would house a population of 5,000, nurturing a sense of community and frugality within its uniquely designed high-density dwellings. There would be no need for cars – everything would be within walking distance. In fact, the city wouldn't even have streets. Instead, it would resemble a colossal horseshoe-shaped stadium with the bulk of the city's accommodation towering over it. Soleri described the philosophy behind his desert city as 'arcology', a melding of architecture and ecology.

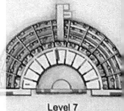

Level 7
PLAN
Scale 1:500

AN URBAN LABORATORY

For many in the West, a detached suburban house remains a key status symbol – the more remote from neighbours the better. Soleri saw this as a detachment from our natural need for community, and one that was contributing to our growing sense of isolation.

> 'Instead of people gathering to develop a culture, they want to escape from other people. Individuals believe they can reach a level of self-sufficiency that can isolate them – or their family – in an ideal place. Then they somehow expect the civilisation that has made them to serve them. It's a parasitic kind of life.'
> –*The Urban Ideal* (2001)

Soleri believed our social ills could be resolved through compact and efficient design. Just as technology moves towards miniaturization and nature evolves into ever more complex organisms, he proposed that human habitation was a 'living organism', which must follow the same process:

> 'Designed for human intercourse and discourse, the city is our appropriate habitat. We must all live communally, to learn from each other. It is the path to compassion.'

To articulate his vision he decided to build up, not out, eschewing the unwieldy urban sprawl that 'wastes time and energy transporting people, goods and services over their expanses'. Along with a bevy of volunteers, he started to craft free-form arches and domes by building mounds of soil, pouring concrete over the top and then hewing out the earth beneath using a technique he called 'earthcasting'.

His city would embrace low-energy, low-tech principles. Those giant concrete apses would be positioned to absorb heat in winter and provide shade in summer. 'Our cities of the future,' Soleri wrote, 'will be integrated ecosystems, dense megastructures that grow their own food and produce their own energy and consciousness. They will be environmentally responsible.'

ENTER THROUGH THE GIFT SHOP

Work on Arcosanti began in 1970, with eager interns shovelling

Paolo Soleri –
you can't fault this
man's ambition!

earth and mixing concrete in the sweltering heat in return
for Soleri's teachings. Before long, strange structures with
porthole windows began to appear on the desert skyline. In
1976, *Newsweek* magazine hailed Arcosanti 'the most important
experiment in urban architecture undertaken in our lifetime'.
As enthusiasm grew, residents moved in, children were born and
concerts were held in its 500-capacity amphitheatre. Workshops,
a kiln, bakery, swimming pool and cafeteria were all built using
goodwill (and lashings of concrete).

By the 1980s, 7,000 volunteers had helped the city reach only
5 per cent of its planned potential; the dream was beginning to
curdle. Soleri's refusal to allow any investors into Arcosanti, for
fear of his vision being compromised, left the project without
any serious funding. The little revenue generated came through
the sale of bronze bells, designed exclusively by Soleri, in its gift
shop. What's more, the community-focused architect now lived
outside of the city in his prototype eco-home Cosanti, surrounded
by wind chimes. Stagnation set in; over the next few decades,
building all but ground to a halt and Arcosanti's population
remained below 100.

Soleri died in 2013, doubtless feeling his life's ambition had

been thwarted. His city of the future now looks very much like a city of the past – part 1960s university campus, part 1950s sci-fi movie set. But before we write Soleri off as a failure, let's not forget, he did try to build an entire city. Hats off to the man!

During the second half of the 20th century, many utopians – including Disney – dreamed of building a futuristic city. None of them did, put off by the sheer scale, cost and ridiculous ambition of it all. All except Soleri, who at least got part of the way there. What's more he built one with modest materials and means, and single-mindedly pursued his ideology into his nineties.

Interestingly, as the dust settles on Arcosanti, Soleri's ideas are enjoying somewhat of a revival. Leonardo DiCaprio interviewed him for the 2007 planet-saving documentary *The 11th Hour,* alongside 70 other renowned thinkers, scientists and Nobel Peace Prize winners, and *Guardian* journalists were tapping the ecotect's earthcast door until the last years of his life. Perhaps this desert-dwelling 'eccentric' was just ahead of his time?

Soleri hated being called a utopian; he preferred to think of himself as an uncompromising realist. As everyday people (and town planners) start to take note of climate change and the importance of low-energy living, our congested, flood-prone, horizontally built suburbs don't seem quite so appealing. Soleri is fast becoming a voice of reason. DB

L.L. ZAMENHOF

The utopian who invented a new world language

In the comedy sci-fi *The Hitchhiker's Guide to the Galaxy* (1978), reluctant protagonist Arthur Dent is given a Babel Fish by his friend Ford Prefect. Once popped in his ear, the fish enables Dent to understand alien languages from every corner of the universe. With a wry humour typical of author Douglas Adams, we later discover that 'in effectively removing all barriers to communication between different races and cultures, (it) has caused more and bloodier wars than anything else in the history of creation'.

One hundred and fifty years ago, back on Earth, Adams' cynicism would have been as welcome as a Vogon poem to Ludwik Lejzer Zamenhof. Born in Poland in 1859, the schoolboy Zamenhof dreamed of creating a new world language to bring humanity closer to world peace. His international language would be phonetic, **simple to learn**, with no convoluted rules for tenses or the absurdities of masculine and feminine nouns. No more 'i before e except after c' nonsense or trying to fathom why the French deem 'hair' to be masculine but 'head' feminine.

Zamenhof grew up to become an ophthalmologist by trade. Being a clever bugger, he was also a zealous linguaphile who learned to speak over a dozen languages. Growing up in an outpost of the Russian Empire, he found his linguistic dexterity to be tremendously useful. Zamenhof had long perceived language barriers to be a common cause of conflict and misunderstanding between his friends and neighbours. While his own family conversed in Yiddish and Polish, his neighbours spoke everything from Russian to Lithuanian and German. In a 1914 letter to a new organization of Jewish Esperantists, Zamenhof wrote that he was 'profoundly convinced that every nationalism offers humanity only the greatest unhappiness'.

Zamenhof was not, however, the first to dream of a unifying world language. In 1879, Johann Martin Schleyer, a German priest, constructed Volapük, which attracted interest and enthusiasm across Europe. All was going well until Schleyer set up the Volapük Academy, promptly fell out with its newly elected French director (doubtlessly over a rogue umlaut) and, in the ensuing bickering, Volapük fell into disuse.

Regardless of the language's fate, Zamenhof had been unimpressed with Volapük. He saw it as convoluted and messy and would later deride it in his own artificial language by using the word *volapukaio* to mean gibberish.

In 1887, after years of burning the midnight oil, Zamenhof published a 44-page booklet entitled *Dr Esperanto's International Language*. And while Esperanto, which translates as 'one who hopes', was only intended as Zamenhof's pen-name, it was eventually adopted as **the name of his new language**.

In his booklet, Zamenhof laid out the rules for his new language and renounced all ownership, declaring it to be 'common property' – thus creating an early form of open-source language. It was an immediate success. Magazines and formal organizations supporting Esperanto sprung up, and by 1905

With only 16 rules of grammar, Zamenhof's language can be picked up by most people in a matter of months. One notable exception is the character Arnold Rimmer in *Red Dwarf*, who has been unsuccessfully learning it for several million years.

This could only be a good thing; International Language was about as boring as calling your pet hamster, 'Hamster'.

the first world congress for Esperanto was held in France. The League of Nations came teasingly close to adopting Esperanto as its primary language and it would come to be championed by such literary giants as Tolstoy, Tolkien and GB Shaw.

UNU LINGVO NENIAM ESTAS SUFICA

Zamenhof dedicated much of his life to establishing the credentials of Esperanto and died in 1917, ever hopeful that it would become a world language. Perhaps it was a blessing he died when he did. While one of the purposes of Esperanto was to liberate its speakers from the politics of established languages, Esperanto fell foul to totalitarian regimes. Hitler denounced it as being part of the Jewish conspiracy while Stalin, who had once been a fan, turned against it in his growing paranoia, describing it as a 'language of spies'. Ironically, after the Second World War, two of Esperanto's biggest supporters were Mao Tse Tung and the Ayatollah Khomeini, both of whom embraced it as a language that was anti-imperialist.

Esperanto reached its peak popularity in the 1960s with the release of four albums and two movies, *Agonies* (1964) and *Incubus* (1966), all in Esperanto. The latter, a black-and-white horror film, stars a young William Shatner as a pious young soldier seduced by an evil succubus. Those who delight in Shatner's intense acting style will be richly rewarded in seeking this film out.

While Zamenhof's dream of a new world language didn't come to fruition, Esperanto is far from dead. With a resurgence of interest owing mainly to the Internet, current estimates reckon it is **spoken by over a million people worldwide**. Online courses are increasingly popular, while Esperanto Wikipedia features over 200,000 entries. And while Zamenhof remains far from a household name, it's comforting to know that he is worshipped as a minor deity by the Oomoto religion in Japan, for 'bringing to Earth a language that is spoken in heaven'. In an age where the artificial languages of Entish, Dothraki and Klingon can now be studied at degree level, Zamenhof remains '*la supro banano*'. DB

With little scope for puns and innuendo, you might think it would be hard to tell a joke in Esperanto. Not so, due to the language's open-ended vocabulary construction, which allows you to freely tack on suffixes to form new words. Take, for example: '*Kial girafo neniam estas sola? Car gi havas kolegon!*' (Why is a giraffe never alone? Because it has a kolego!) A *koleg'o* means a colleague, while a *kol'eg'o* translates as a big (-eg-) neck (kol-). See what we mean?

MADALYN MURRAY O'HAIR

The most hated woman in America

'No one was really surprised when she was eventually murdered,' John Waters writes of his hero Madalyn Murray O'Hair in his 2011 book *Role Models*. For decades, she was had been a thorn in the side of America's religious Right.

She got death threats smeared in human faeces from foaming-at-the-mouth religious fanatics, furious about her attempts to rid America of the 'poison' of Christianity. In an interview with *Life* magazine in 1963, she said: 'I think sooner or later some night some nut is going to get a message from Jesus Christ and I'm going to have had it.' But in the end Madalyn Murray O'Hair, the irrepressible foul-mouthed leader of godless America, was done in by a threat much closer to home.

O'Hair's atheist campaign kicked off in autumn 1960 at

a high school in Baltimore. Her son William had just started the term and, like most other public schools in the United States, here children were expected to say morning prayers and read the Bible. But the O'Hair family were what were euphemistically known then as 'non-believers' and Madalyn was disgusted when she saw rows of kids with their heads bowed, mumbling prayers in unison. Not only were her son's rights to non-belief being ignored, she thought, the State was taking taxes to train ranks of unquestioning religious drones. 'It's un-American and unconstitutional,' she raged, and promptly filed a petition against the city of Baltimore to have prayer and Bible reading banned from its public school system.

It was a bad time to be an atheist in America. The Soviet Union had proudly declared its freedom from religion so, to set itself apart from those 'commie bastards', the United States painted itself as the most god-fearing country in the Western world. In 1954, the government changed the wording of the Pledge of Allegiance from 'one nation, indivisible, with liberty and justice for all' to 'one nation, under God' (with liberty and justice for most, so long as they believed in God). Just in case there were any lingering doubts about whether or not God was pumped up about American capitalism, in 1955 'In God We Trust' was added to US currency. Put this God-bothering together with the McCarthy witch trials and you've got a stiflingly conservative society where conformity is the order of the day.

So mainstream America wasn't going to take too kindly to this obnoxious, atheist single mother of two sons born out of wedlock. She was swiftly fired from her job and spat at in the street. Every window of her house was broken and the death threats started to roll in.

When the Baltimore courts denied her petition, it must hardly have seemed worth it. But O'Hair wasn't the kind of woman who takes no for an answer. She appealed to the US Supreme Court and, in an unprecedented decision, the Court ruled that yes – prayer and Bible study in schools was unconstitutional. O'Hair had won her first and most remarkable victory. America hated her for it.

She didn't stop there. Now infamous across the States, O'Hair used her fame to launch a series of campaigns – suing NASA for allowing astronauts to read the Bible on live TV, taking the city of Baltimore to court for failing to collect taxes from the Catholic Church and setting up the American Atheists association, which still exists to promote and defend the rights of non-believers in America. She even wrote speeches for that other bogeyman of the moral majority, *Hustler*'s Larry Flynt.

A CHAMPION OF FREETHINKING

For more than 30 years, Madalyn Murray O'Hair was the loudest dissenting voice in an America that was more and more 'under God', until one day in August 1995 she suddenly fell silent. Kidnapped and held hostage for weeks, Madalyn, her son Jon and granddaughter Robin were finally strangled, dismembered and dumped in a shallow grave outside San Antonio, Texas. Despite what everyone assumed, her murder was committed not by a religious nut, but by a disgruntled former employee out to steal the family's savings. But maybe it makes little difference if you're killed for God or you're killed for money in a country whose legal tender bears the motto 'In God We Trust'.

O'Hair cared more about social justice and politics than atheism. Her lifelong crusade stemmed from a belief that it was an American's responsibility to question authority, to confront conformity and defy groupthink. An atheist, an anarchist and a feminist, above all O'Hair was a champion of freethinking and free speech: there's a video from the 1970s on YouTube where she says, 'If we can question the ultimate authority, God – who must be obeyed – then we can question the authority of the State, the university structure, our employer…'

In an age where bland conformity is once again on the rise and populist politics seems to be taking over, Madalyn Murray O'Hair reminds us 'to strive for intellectual freedom, not mental bondage; to seek joy, not sorrow; love not fear'. This 'you can do… only when you realize who and what your oppressor was – and is'. *DH*

THOMAS MIDGLEY JR.

The worst inventor in history

As a polio-stricken Thomas Midgley Jr. lay entangled in the strings and pulleys of the hoist mechanism he'd invented to help him out of bed, what final images flashed through his mind? Hospitalized factory workers neurologically crippled by lead poisoning? Satellite pictures of a gaping hole in the ozone layer? Probably not. It seems the gifted but misguided engineer and chemist vacated this planet with little inclination of the damage he'd done to it. How could one man get it so, so wrong? Twice!

Midgley was born 18 May 1889 in Pennsylvania. His father was an inventor and, as a boy fascinated by gadgetry and science, Thomas was determined to follow in his father's footsteps. The young Midgley showed innovation from a young age, devising a way of giving his high school baseball enough slipperiness for maximum curve by using an extract of bark from a slippery elm. Also known as 'spitball', the practice is deemed illegal in baseball today. Perhaps a sign of things to come in Midgley's career.

He graduated from Cornell University in 1911 with a degree in mechanical engineering and embarked on his profession designing cash registers before joining his father in the development of car tyres and parts. Showing an affinity for motor engines, Midgley then joined the research staff of Dayton Engineering Laboratories Company. He was a model employee, working long hours and overcoming obstacles with creative, and often daring, methods. When a spark plug blew up in his face and embedded shrapnel in his eye, the obvious solution for Midgley was to bathe it in mercury and float the tiny pieces out himself.

Soon his superiors would entrust him with a research project that would gain him recognition in the field of chemistry, as well as engineering. It was to solve the problem of engine knock –

a noise made by engines that indicated a loss of power from rapid ignition. Midgley tested thousands of compounds to reduce the knock, including some unlikely materials, such as melted butter.

One winter, upon noticing a plant with red leaves continuing to grow under snow, Midgley surmised that the colour red absorbs more radiant heat and, when added to fuel, would evaporate more completely – thus preventing rough combustion. As a result, he added iodine into his experiments. It proved a triumph and the knocking almost completely stopped – although he soon realized this was because of the chemical properties of iodine increasing the octane rating of the fuel, rather than the colour.

Stretching his legs as a chemist, Midgley began experimenting with more effective additives than iodine and soon hit upon a formulation of lead called tetraethyl lead (TEL) – a mixture of bromoethane and chloroethane. It worked a treat, eliminating engine knock completely. Its name was simplified to ethyl.

The inventor unveiled his discovery with an air of showmanship, firing up a spluttering engine in the middle of Carnegie Hall then blowing a tiny whiff of ethyl at the carburetor and instantly silencing the knock. And that was that. The motor companies had their prized fuel additive, which was then pumped through the engines of millions of cars and aircraft around the world.

The toxicity of this new substance was, however, immediately noticed and generated alarming reports among the media. In response, Midgley assembled the press, soaked his hands in ethyl and inhaled it for 60 seconds. He failed to report that it took him a year to recover from the poisoning. Meanwhile, General Motor's ethyl plant was forced to close when several workers went mad and died. Ethyl had a new nickname – 'looney gas'.

MEASURING THE CONSEQUENCES

It wasn't until the 1950s, long after Midgley's death, that the disastrous impact of lead gasoline would be realized. Clair Patterson, a young geochemist from Iowa was examining ice core samples from Greenland and noticed that lead isotopes were significantly higher in the last few decades. The reason? Leaded gas in our engines. In the 1970s and 1980s, there were alarming reports that increased levels of lead in the atmosphere were doing irreversible damage to infants, who were more likely to grow up to have behavioural issues, commit crime and become drug addicts. The Environmental Protection Agency launched an investigation, leading to the banning of leaded gasoline around the world, although it is still used in high-octane aviation fuels and in some developing countries to this day.

Midgley, however, wasn't done making his mark. He moved on to the second big problem he wanted to solve. He was called upon to find a non-flammable, non-toxic refrigerant, and he quickly discovered something to fit the bill – dichlorodifluoromethane, the first chloroflouro-carbon (CFC), consisting of fluorine, carbon and chlorine. Never one to shy away from using his body as a human test dummy, he demonstrated the refrigerant's non-toxicity and fireproof properties by inhaling a lungful to blow out a candle. Again, his discovery met with huge success and CFCs were soon used in anything that required inert gas, from air conditioners and refrigerators to aerosols and asthma inhalers.

It would take decades for us to notice the build-up of these synthetic chemicals. In 1973, haunting pictures from space showed gaping holes in the Earth's ozone layer. Chemists Frank Rowland and Mario Molina discovered it was CFC molecules doing the damage and they were called to testify before Congress, leading to the banning of CFCs internationally in 1987. Since then, scientists have projected that global ozone will return to normal levels by 2080, which seems an alarmingly long way off.

Midgley's career continued along the upward trajectory of accolades, awards and respectful pats on the back right up until he contracted polio and found himself wheelchair bound. He designed a contraption to help him out of bed but, on 2 November 1944, got entangled in the cords and pulleys and strangled himself to death – the third of his inventions to go tragically wrong.

Undoubtedly, Midgley was a bright and innovative scientist but clearly not a conscientious one. By purporting the safety of ethyl, he was reckless in the extreme – he must have known about its high toxicity levels because of the bouts of illness he suffered. And when it comes to global warming and climate change, there can be little doubt that Midgley is responsible for some of the human race's most catastrophic effects on the environment. *AW*

DR JAMES GRAHAM

The world's first sexologist

Picture a bed designed to create the ultimate erotic experience for any couple that copulates on it. It stands 12 feet by 9 feet (3.7m × 2.7m), canopied by an enormous dome adorned with the entwined figures of Hymen and Psyche, holding aloft a flaming torch. Musical automata perform around the edge of the dome, while inside a reservoir emits a heady blend of oriental essences. Beneath, a silk-laden mattress stuffed with the hair of English stallions lies on an inner frame that can be tilted for prime sexual positioning, while the gyrations of the couple activate celestial sounds from glass organ pipes. To top it off, the entire bed is electrically charged and underlaid with magnets.

It may sound like the far-fetched concoction of a mediocre sci-fi, fantasy and erotic novelist, but this celestial bed was in fact the creation of James Graham, an 18th-century sexologist who championed the health benefits of magnetism and electricity, particularly for the curing of sexual problems.

Graham was born 23 June 1745 in Edinburgh. The son of a saddler, he studied medicine at the University of Edinburgh – patronized by the eminent physician William Buchan, author of one of the most widely referenced medical books at the time. Failing to complete his studies, the impetuous young man headed to America, where he witnessed the electrical experiments of Benjamin Franklin. Graham was hooked. He became obsessed with the effects of electricity on the human body, believing it could reinvigorate flaccid and defunct organs into robust vigour:

'Electricity is the most powerful engine or influence in nature to remedy these several defects: it gives a tone to the lax fibres – it corrects the acrimony of the juices by increasing the

perspiration, strengthens the animal powers, and effectually removes obstructions.'
–James Graham, *Medical Transactions at the Temple of Health* (1782)

He returned to England and set up a practice in Bath, specializing in therapies to help with infertility and impotence by applying 'Effluvia, Vapours and Applications aetherial, magnetic or electric'. He couldn't have chosen a better time – electricity and mechanical apparatus being the height of fashion, the thrilling new sciences of the Enlightenment.

It was while practising in Bath that Graham was endorsed by his first celebrity patient, Catherine Macauley, a renowned historian recently widowed. She married Graham's younger brother William, 20 years her junior, and the ensuing gossip about her sexual reawakening pushed Graham and his wonder treatments into the limelight.

Graham gained enough confidence and capital to see through his vision, opening a Temple of Health in the Adelphi, London, in 1770. For a two-guinea entrance fee, visitors could enter this palace of enchantment, inhale perfumed air, hear otherworldly music, explore Graham's medico-electric apparatus and encounter his beautiful Goddesses of Health, posing in Grecian robes.

From his Temple of Health, Graham gave public lectures on the virtues of sexual health and personal hygiene, recommending the cold washing of the genitals after sex, in order to

'lock the cock and secure all for the next rencontre' and improve the condition of the testicles, which 'next morning after a laborious night would be relaxed, lank, and pendulous, like the two dead eyes of a sheep dangling in a wet empty calf's bladder...'
–James Graham, 1782 pamplet

Graham also encouraged foreplay – believing conception to be a momentous act that required momentous sensations for a 'sublime orgasm'. Sublime was his favourite word – he used it often.

THE TEMPLE OF HYMEN
At the height of his popularity, Graham decided it was time

DR. GRAHAM'S
CELESTIAL BED
AT THE TEMPLE OF HYMEN, PALL MALL, ANNO DOMINI 1782

Cartoonist, engineer and automaton inventor Tim Hunkin sketches out his vision of Dr Graham's Celestial Bed.

to open another palace of pleasure – the Temple of Hymen at Schomberg House on Pall Mall, London. It was here that he installed his 'wonder-working edifice', the Celestial Bed, charging aristocratic couples, desperate to conceive an heir, the mighty sum of £50 a night. Keen to uphold a moral code and deter any unmarrieds or adulterers, he had the words '*Procul! O procul este Profane*' inscribed above the entrance to the Temple, translating 'Begone, begone ye uninitiated'.

Despite the lucrative bed rental fee, the temple was an expensive venture that landed Graham in debt. It soon degraded into a brothel, and Graham fled to Edinburgh, turning his back on sex therapy to extol the life-giving benefits of mud bathing. He believed that mud held the secret to immortality, for the body could absorb all the nutrients necessary to sustain life.

By 1786, he was back in London, in Panton Street, Soho, giving public lectures while buried up to his neck in earth. His behaviour grew ever more eccentric – he founded a new Church and became a religious fanatic, undressing in the street to give his clothing to passers-by and subjecting himself to extreme fasting. After a spell in an asylum and a prolonged bout of fasting, James Graham died in Edinburgh in 1794.

During his lifetime, Graham had many very vocal critics for whom he trod a fine line between respectability and ridicule. William Wordsworth called him 'the great high priest' while others dismissed him as an 'emperor of quacks'. A 1783 caricature, published at the height of his fame, depicts him lecturing an audience with the caption 'How Fluent Nonsense Trickles from his Tongue'.

Despite his eccentricities, perhaps these are unfair portrayals of a well-intentioned man? In many ways, Graham was a pioneer of marriage guidance. He gave sound advice to emotionally and physically estranged clients, much of it highly modern and forward-thinking, such as his advocating healthier diets, fresh air and enjoyable sex for both man and wife. He encouraged couples to spend more time together and see each other in fresh, more attractive lights. Perhaps this, not an electrified bed, should be his legacy. AW

SEEKERS' DIRECTORY

FRANCIS GALTON

PODCAST *Odditorium* podcast, series 1, episode 11: *Eugenics and Tea* (2015), Dan Maier – oddpodcast.com

BOOK Martin Brookes, *Extreme Measures: The Dark Visions and Bright Ideas of Francis Galton* (2004)

FLORA TRISTAN

BOOK Flora Tristan, *The Peregrinations of a Pariah* (1838)

BOOK Flora Tristan, *The Workers' Union* (1843)

BOOK Charles Neilson Gatter, *Gauguin's Astonishing Grandmother: Flora Tristan* (1970)

ELAINE MORGAN

TED TALK Elaine Morgan, *I Believe We Evolved from Aquatic Apes* (2009)

BOOKS Elaine Morgan, *The Descent of Woman* (1972), *The Aquatic Ape Hypothesis* (1997)

RADIO DOCUMENTARY 'The Scars of Evolution' (2005), presented by David Attenborough, BBC Radio 4

BUCKMINSTER FULLER

BOOK Buckminster Fuller, *Operating Manual for Spaceship Earth* (1968)

FIELD TRIP Find your local geodesic domes: Eden Project, Cornwall; Montreal biosphere; the Matr Mandir globe, Auroville, India.

DOCUMENTARY *The World of Buckminster Fuller* (1974)

MAP Treat yourself to a Woodcut Dymaxion Map (the winning entry in a design competition hosted by the Buckminster Fuller Institute) – bfi.org

RESOURCE Connect with fellow inventors, entrepreneurs and archivists inspired by Fuller's ideas at the Buckminster Fuller Institute – bfi.org

JOHN HUNTER

BOOK Hilary Mantel, *The Giant, O'Brien* (2010)

OPERA *The Odditorium* contributor Sarah Angliss has written a new opera, *Giant* (2016), based on the life and death of Charles Byrne – sarahangliss.com

FIELD TRIP Visit the Hunterian Museum (*above*) where, among a crocodile foetus, cockerel's head complete with human tooth and a myriad of surgical instruments, you'll find the remains of Charles Byrne – hunterianmuseum.org

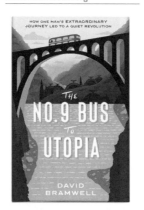

HOW ONE MAN'S EXTRAORDINARY JOURNEY LED TO A QUIET REVOLUTION

THE NO.9 BUS TO UTOPIA

DAVID BRAMWELL

PAOLO SOLERI

FIELD TRIP Visit the city of Arcosanti in Arizona, US. Join a five-week workshop, watch Shakespeare and jazz in the amphitheater and buy a wind chime – arcosanti.org

BOOK Paolo Soleri, *The Urban Ideal* (2001)

BOOK David Bramwell, *The No.9 Bus to Utopia* (2014)

DOCUMENTARY *The 11th Hour* (2007)

L.L. ZAMENHOF

FILM *Incubus* featuring William Shatner (1966), a black-and-white horror film in Esperanto

POETRY Read the work of William Auld, who wrote prolifically in Esperanto and was nominated for the Nobel Prize in Literature.

MADALYN MURRAY O'HAIR

BOOK Madalyn Murray O'Hair, *What on Earth is an Atheist* (2004)

THOMAS MIDGELEY JUNIOR

BIOGRAPHY Charles F. Kettering, *Biographical Memoir of Thomas Midgley Jr* (1947)

BOOK Bill Bryson, *A Short History of Nearly Everything* (2004)

TV SERIES *QI*, Divination episode, Series D (2006), BBC

DR JAMES GRAHAM

FIELD TRIP If you love politically incorrect contraptions, head to Tim Hunkin's wonderful Novelty Automation in Holborn, London – novelty-automation.com

BOOK Lydia Syson, *Doctor of Love: James Graham & His Celestial Bed* (2012)

5

EXPLORERS OF THE MIND

Given Fig. 2, also C N drawn through V, & C M through P, where
C P = E F, –

5

EXPLORERS OF THE MIND

In 1900, Lord Kelvin, addressing an assembly of physicists at the British Association for the Advancement of Science, solemnly declared: 'There is nothing new to be discovered in physics now. All that remains is more and more precise measurement.' Had he lived another 20 years, Kelvin would have doubtless been kicking himself when the very bedrock of science was shaken by Einstein's theory of relativity and by quantum mechanics. The universe, and everything in it, was proving to be far stranger and more elusive than we could possibly have imagined. Reality really did seem to be all in the mind. Or, as writer Anaïs Nin perceptively put it: 'We don't see things as they are, we see things as we are.'

Along with quantum theory, the pioneering work of Jung and Freud instigated a psychological and cultural shift in the 20th century from the outer world to the inner. It is for this reason that this final chapter is firmly rooted in the last 100 years, exploring the ideas of some of the psychic adventurers who rode the shockwaves of counterculture, psychedelia, psychoanalysis and post-modernism. By the 1980s, writer

South

D

Given Fig. 2, also C N drawn through V, & C M through P, where CP = EF, –

Joseph Campbell would observe: 'In the 20th century we have dismantled our old myths because they no longer serve us. What we need are new myths to live by.'

Plenty stepped forward to fill the void. Occultist Aleister Crowley and author Ayn Rand were both proponents of Objectivism – the need to release ourselves from the will of others (looking after number one). Psychologist Wilhelm Reich saw sexual liberation as a means to free humanity. For Timothy Leary, salvation lay in liberal doses of LSD, while, for Robert Anton Wilson and Alan Watts, the ultimate struggle was to liberate ourselves from all our 'reality tunnels'. They even made it sound fun.

By the 1960s, the rise of the New Age inspired unprecedented interest in the transformation of consciousness. When George Harrison sang on 'Inner Light', 'Without going out of my door, I can know all things on Earth,' he inadvertently predicted our Internet-dominated future. As we journey through the 21st century, our profound relationship with the natural world has shifted towards an intimacy with and dependence on a virtual realm. We are now connected through a vast, external nervous system – a digital network that is everywhere and nowhere. Whether we like it or not, we inhabit a new inner universe of our own creation.

At his trial, shortly before his death, Socrates declared: 'The unexamined life is not worth living.' We may still climb mountains, surf tidal bores and pass ourselves off as Tibetan lamas but, ultimately, it is only through journeying into the exotic landscapes of the mind that we can truly come to understand ourselves.

N
M
P
L

North

B

Given Fig. 2, also CN drawn through V, & CM through P, where CP = EF, –

FALCO TARASSACO

The Italian time lord

In the foothills of the Alps, an hour's drive north of Turin, lies the eighth wonder of the world: the Temples of Humankind. A vast underground network, equivalent in size to St Paul's Cathedral, it boasts nine chambers, secret stairways, a labyrinth and a pyramidal glass music hall. These colourful, cavernous buildings, decorated in parts with Egyptian symbology, were constructed over two decades by Damanhur, a spiritual community led by a man called Falco Tarassaco (which translates as Hawk Dandelion).

The Temples of Humankind are a genuinely astonishing architectural wonder. While all of the world's great ancient

monuments are past their best, weathered by nature and history, here the paint is still drying. And yet, despite being the world's most ambitious work of outsider art, chances are you've never heard of the Temples of Humankind which, quite frankly, are as bizarre as the story of their creator.

Damanhur was founded in the summer of 1978, when 30 like-minded people were brought to an Alpine mountainside by their spiritual leader, Falco Tarassaco. He instructed them to build a temple, 'the like of which has not been seen for thousands of years'. They begin to dig in secret, at night.

For the next 13 years, in an operation that would have made the building of the Tom, Dick and Harry tunnels in *The Great Escape* seem like child's play, two million buckets of rock, earth and clay were removed from the mountain. By 1991, they had completed eight separate temples, which boasted marble floors, stained-glass ceilings, mosaics, carved columns and statues.

The Damanhurians (a community that now numbered 134)

were careful to cover their tracks, knowing that they didn't have planning permission. But after a former member tried to blackmail them, they came clean to the Italian authorities in 1992. In 1995, after press campaigns, Internet appeals and a petition, the buildings were declared to be a unique work of art. With a few health and safety tweaks, the installation of a lift and the obligatory gift shop, the Temples of Humankind were allowed to remain in the hands of their citizens, earning a place in the *Guinness Book of Records* as the World's Largest Underground Temple (although, to be honest, there's little competition in this category).

Along with the temples, the community went on to build a village with an open temple (Damjl) and schools, and even convert an Olivetti factory into workshops, a supermarket and conference hall. Nowadays, Damanhur has a population of nearly 1,000, who live in communal houses called *nucleos*. The community makes money through its GM-free organic produce and by constructing eco-houses. Although Tarassaco passed away in 2013, his extraordinary time on Earth lives on through a community that describes itself as 'a laboratory for the future of humankind'.

But who was Falco Tarassaco and why did he urge his followers to spend decades creating a vast underground temple? Hold on to your hat, we're taking a journey far into the future!

It's AD 2600 (or thereabouts) and the Earth has been destroyed by alien terrorists who, in an act of malicious nihilism, have removed humankind's free will and sent the planet on a path of destruction. Observing this all from a corner of the

galaxy is a group of interplanetary delegates who meet every Friday as part of some current affairs panel. One of them has a fondness for the people of Earth and decides to save us. He travels back in time to 1950 and has himself 'pre-incarnated' into the body of a human baby in Turin, named Oberto Airaudi.

At a young age, Airaudi realizes his mission in life is to save humanity from destruction. After spending his early twenties as an insurance salesman, he gets down to the job in hand – amassing a small group of followers and encouraging them to help him build a giant battery to jolt the Earth on to a new timeline.

However, in order to do this, the team first need to locate the Earth's 'synchronic knot' (a meeting point of the planet's four 'rivers of energy'). Had it been in Central Park or under the Kremlin, Airaudi would have been scuppered but, as luck would have it (and after travelling the world), he discovers that it's actually less than an hour's drive from Turin. Better still, the land is for sale.

The group establishes a small community, Damanhur (Egyptian for City of Light), and members begin to **adopt animal and plant names**. Oberto Airaudi becomes Falco Tarassaco. The giant battery they are building, dug into a rare but highly conductive rock strata known as mylonite, will eventually become known as the Temples of Humankind.

After completing the temples and conducting a number of complex rituals, the team manages to create a new timeline and the planet is saved. And while Tarassaco and the odd companion have to travel back to Atlantis occasionally to buy essential nuts and bolts from a specialist timeline hardware store, humanity's free will is restored and once again we have the power to decide the planet's fate.

Once they have accomplished certain goals for the community and themselves, all residents exchange their name for one made up of a plant and animal, adopting names such as Ant Coriander or Sunset Butterfly Pineapple. Some, like Sponge Strawberry or Swordfish Banana, could be mistaken for Jamie Oliver recipes.

THE 'MYTH' OF DAMANHUR

While the Temples of Humankind are – in the true sense of the word – awesome, anyone travelling to Damanhur seeking evidence of aliens and time travel might be disappointed. Visitors might also have been surprised by Tarassaco. He could often be spotted around the community, and was no slouch when it came to sharing communal duties. But where other spiritual gurus have classically favoured pony tails, white robes and tie-dye trousers, Tarassaco seemed to be permanently attired in jeans and a zip-up cardigan –

more part-time lecturer in computer studies than alien superhero. On a Friday evening, he conducted interviews and visitors could ask him anything they liked. However, anyone asking such direct questions as: 'Are you an alien?' would be met with a grin and a vague answer such as: 'I'm merely someone trying to do their best.'

To dismiss Tarassaco as a charlatan who convinced his followers to build a spiritual theme park is, however, to miss the point of Damanhur entirely. In his TV series *The Power of Myth*, writer Joseph Campbell (see later in this chapter) discusses how our old religions and myths 'no longer serve us' – which is why, in the West at least, they are being abandoned. But, as Campbell argues, while science is the best language we have for explaining the universe, what the world needs right now are 'modern myths' to teach us how to live.

In recent decades, Hollywood has articulated new modern myths, such as *Star Wars*, but what Tarassaco has created with Damanhur appears to be utterly unique in the modern world – a living myth. His is a modern-day parable that weaves time travel, terrorism and Egyptian symbology with environmental concerns and the destruction of the Earth. With Airaudi as auteur, Damanhur's residents built a glorious film set on an epic scale, chose their roles and – year by year – continue to develop the script. Tarassaco, understandably, kept the best role for himself: a spiritual Dr Who.

We'll never really know how much Tarassaco believed his own myth, but does it really matter? Thanks to his singular vision, the world's largest underground temple is now lodged inside an Alpine mountain – open to visitors for a modest entrance fee. The gift shop needs a bit of attention, but you can't have everything. Plus, this is no dusty pile of stone but a living temple, regularly used for Damanhurian rituals and ceremonies.

In contemplating Falco Tarassaco's life and his impact on our world, perhaps a more important question we need to ask ourselves is this: when news of the Earth's eighth wonder of the world broke in 1992, why were we all so wrapped up in the misery and paranoia of daily events that one of the most incredible global stories of the last 50 years went unnoticed? DB

*The Temples
of Humankind*
DAMANHUR

1	Entrance	5	Hall of Spheres
2	Blue Temple	6	Hall of Metals
3	Hall of Water	7	Hall of the Earth
4	Hall of Mirrors	8	Labyrinth

AYN RAND

The Russian who sold the American dream to America

Mention the name Ayn Rand on most shores and you'll probably get a quizzical shrug, coupled with an 'Ann who'? For starters, it's Ayn – as in 'mine' – which is apt, as we shall see.

Stateside it's a different story as, some 34 years after her death, Rand – the author and founder of Objectivism – continues to make many a head revolve. There, she is simultaneously reviled and worshipped, with famous devotees to her turbo-charged 'to thine own self be true' philosophy ranging from Penn Jillette (of magicians Penn and Teller) and Martina Navratilova (who enjoyed Rand's novel *The Fountainhead* (1943) and its 'striving for excellence' message) to Tea Party politician Paul Ryan. Hell, even Canadian prog-rocking giants Rush were obsessed by Rand, with drummer/lyricist Neil Peart **name-checking the Russian firebrand** as inspiration for the fantastically nutty 1976 album *2112*, which contained a bizarre sci-fi plot apparently based on Rand's novella *Anthem*.

Flip the dime and there's a healthy queue of **righteously indignant people ready to shout down** what some call her infantile ideas and 'zero-empathy' perspective, not to mention her clunkily written books. She did, however, make an undeniable impact on the American psyche. Indeed, in today's political climate, she appears to be achieving a posthumous vindication. But let's get some context.

Born Alicia Rosenbaum, Rand was a fiercely independent émigree with a steel-trap mind and an unwieldy ego who escaped the Bolshevik-led St Petersburg in 1926 and made her way to the United States, where the glittering skyscrapers were 'the will of man made visible'. Determined to kick-start her very own American dream, **Rand changed her name** as soon as she hit the promised land.

It's important to note that witnessing the Red Guard ransacking her father's pharmacy, then the consequent whittling away of her family's considerable fortune, was a pivotal moment in Rand's development. Seeing her father's torment as the red seal was slapped across the storefront, thereby nationalizing it in the name of the people, was for the 12-year-old a 'horrible, silent spectacle of brutality and injustice' (Howard Koch, *As Time Goes By: Memoir of a Writer* (1979). The legacy was her deep loathing for 'self-sacrifice', which meant giving up independence and spirit to the Soviet state, as well as hard-earned goods and chattels. This attitude transmogrified into a lifelong mistrust of altruism. 'You can't have your cake and let your neighbour eat it too,' says one of her characters in *Atlas Shrugged* (1957).

To Rand, Robin Hood was a true villain, because he took from those who had used their will and wit to gain wealth to give to those who didn't have the discipline, brains or drive to create it for themselves. This was seen as an unconscionable symbol of 'need, not achievement, as the source of rights'.

After stints as a film extra (where she stalked and bagged her long-suffering husband, actor Frank O'Connor) and a script-taster for MGM, she tried her hand at playwriting and then birthed her *magna opera* – *The Fountainhead* and *Atlas Shrugged*.

Architect Howard Roark, the individualistic hero of *The Fountainhead*, doesn't back down from his ideals and blows up a housing project because it's built differently from his design. The

Rush's iconic logo – a naked man opposing the red star – is less of a thumbs-up for nudism and more of a Randian two-finger gesture to the principles of socialism.

In 2013 US comedian and monologuist Mike Daisy performed his show *F*cking F*cking F*cking Ayn Rand* to sell-out crowds. We'll leave you to figure out on which side of the fence he sat.

Apparently Ayn is a Jewish endearment for 'bright eyes', derived from the Hebrew word for 'eye', and her surname was inspired by her Remington Rand typewriter. While nice theories, these have never been substantiated.

mammoth *Atlas Shrugged* evokes a dystopian America where – in reaction to government-led restrictions on their trading rights – society's most successful industrialists, scientists and inventors turn their back on the nation to create their own utopia, causing the collapse of vital industries. In one passage a trainload of passengers suffocate and Rand explains how it's pretty much their fault because they are essentially freeloading from those at the top of the tree.

The 1949 movie of *The Fountainhead*, directed by the legendary King Vidor, is intensely melodramatic, unintentionally entertaining and peppered with steamy moments between blouse-ripping hero Roark (Gary Cooper) and his breast-heaving heroine Dominique (Patricia Neal). Rand, it turns out, had a very specific view of the male/female dynamic when it came to sex – favouring an over-heated 'S&M Mills & Boon' writing style and the depiction of torrid rape-like encounters, where women worship the stubbornness of men who are driven solely by the integrity of their ideals.

THE PURSUIT OF HAPPINESS

By the start of the 1990s, her novels had become a phenomenon in America, favoured by students, politicians and businesspeople. *Atlas Shrugged* was named by a Book of the Month Club survey as the second most influential book in the United States – after the Bible. It's even cited as inspiring the entrepreneurs of Silicon Valley, where new technology could turn everyone into maverick individuals and computer networks could create their own kind of order.

Alongside the writing came her philosophy – Objectivism. A devoted Aristotelian, her central idea was the existence of an objective reality that is separate from consciousness. Rand stated we should use intellect, will and rational skill to live our lives to become 'self-assured creators':

'Man's highest moral purpose is the achievement of his own happiness. We should be free of all forms of political and religious control and live lives guided only by our selfish desires. Each man must live as an end in himself… What does it matter that we're alone? Who do we need? Why do we need anyone?' –Ayn Rand, *For the New Intellectual* (1961)

The opposite of this self-reliance was 'the passive social parasite' or 'moocher'. 'Looters' were those who took money 'by force' (or through taxation). Rand was unsurprisingly a big fan of laissez-faire capitalism and the free markets. Her work influenced key figures including economist Alan Greenspan, who persuaded Bill Clinton to cut government spending and allow the free markets to transform America (but latterly distanced himself from Rand's ideas, deemed impractical).

Inevitably, Rand became engaged in politics, loathing Roosevelt and his socialistic 'New Deal' programmes and expressing frustration with the Conservatives, whose manifestos didn't go far enough.

There are, inevitably, contradictions in Rand's story. Neither Russia nor her family had any real meaning for her because those things were happenstance, not chosen by free will. In her constant claims to having created her own destiny, it was easier then to overlook the fact she was helped by her extended family to get to the States and was supported by relatives on her arrival. Rand famously railed against government handouts and yet allegedly claimed Medicare and social security towards the end of her life. Sadly, she became enslaved to her own 'irrational' emotions at the end of a torrid affair with one of her acolytes, Nathaniel Branden, who was 25 years her junior and dared to reject her. Passionately in love with him, she became violent, jealous and hell-bent on destroying his reputation.

What can't be denied is that Ms Rand was an intensely dynamic trailblazer with a devoted following and remains a divisive figure to this day. Let's leave the last words to Barbara Branden who, despite her husband's affair with Rand, remained a staunch admirer until the rather lonely end of her idol's life:

'Her person encompassed the grandeur of the heroes of her novels, their iron determination, vast intellect and imagination, impassioned pursuit of their goals, courage, pride, and their love of life – her virtues were larger then life... and so were her shortcomings.'
–Barbara Branden, *The Passion of Ayn Rand* (1987). EK

JOHN DEE

The last royal wizard

Nowadays, virtually the only way to achieve academic recognition is to become an expert in a narrowly specialized field. But to be seen as a leading scholar during the Renaissance, you had to be an authority on mathematics, geometry, astronomy, medicine, cryptology, geology, navigation, architecture, law and ancient history, plus, of course, theology, astrology, alchemy and divination – and be able to deliver lectures on any of them in English, French, Latin and ancient Greek. The last man in England who could cover all of those bases lived from 1527 to 1609 – his name was John Dee, the last wizard in England.

As a child prodigy and voracious reader, Dee was packed off to Cambridge University at the age of 15 to study divinity. He worked 18 hours a day, slept four hours a night, graduated at the age of 18 and, by the time he was 19, was a founding fellow of the new Trinity College.

To understand Dee's greatness, we have to appreciate that what we call science and what we think of as hocus-pocus were once equally valued and were often interchangeable. Astrology was usually highly regarded, but mathematics was often seen as a dark art, punishable by death. Dee was arrested for drawing up astrological charts for the princesses Mary and Elizabeth, not for spreading pagan beliefs but for treason. The crime he was charged with was 'calculating'. Mechanical engineering was also suspicious. At Cambridge University, Dee designed the set for a stage production of Aristophanes' play *Peace* and built a mechanical dung beetle that appeared to fly up into the heavens with an actor on its back. For that, Dee was accused of sorcery.

Dee walked the line between currying favour with the monarch of the day, turning down highly paid posts at

Continental universities and pursuing his wildly expensive passions for collecting books, foreign travel, alchemy and maths. He had the misfortune to live through an age of religious turmoil under five monarchs (seven if you count the nine days of Queen Jane and the co-regency of Mary Tudor's husband, Phillip II of Spain).

After the death of Henry VIII, Dee had no sooner won the patronage of the Protestant-raised King Edward VI than the young king was succeeded by the Catholic Mary Tudor, and no sooner had he persuaded her to sponsor his scheme to establish a national library than she died and was succeeded by the founder of the Church of England, Queen Elizabeth I.

Elizabeth proved to be his best ally, however. She even visited him at his home in Mortlake, which became a centre for scholarship and housed the largest library in the land with over 3,000 books and 1,000 manuscripts – more than the university libraries of Oxford and Cambridge combined.

Not only did Dee collect all of these books, he *read* them: books on mathematics, natural history, music, astronomy, military history, cryptography, ancient history and alchemy. We know this because he wrote his name in every one and scribbled meticulous notes in the margins.

John Dee used his astrological skills to set the date of Queen Elizabeth I's coronation, was able to explain to her a new star (a supernova) which suddenly lit up the sky in 1572 and was able to persuade her that she wasn't under a curse when a wax effigy of her had been found in a courtyard stuck with pins. He coined the term 'British Empire' for her, advised her to further England's political and economic interests by setting up colonies in America and reassured her of her legal right to do so. He used his understanding of Euclidean geometry to teach her sea captains to navigate the Arctic in search of the fabled North-West Passage and trade with China (though they failed); he scoured Europe for medical advice to cure her debilitating toothache and even tried to make her rich with tips on where to look for gold.

Unfortunately, the 1,500 tons of black rocks he persuaded Captain Martin Frobisher to risk his life bringing back from Baffin Island in what is today northern Canada turned out to be nothing more than just black rocks. These bankrupted him and

John Dee evoking a spirit of a deceased person with fellow magician Edward Kelley.

made the most costly pile of rubble in Christendom. Some can still be seen patching up a crumbling stone wall that runs the length
of Priory Road in Dartford.

ENTER THE EARLESS MAN

It seems Queen Elizabeth was reluctant to reward Dee for all his hard work, and his expensive book-buying addiction forced him to borrow huge amounts of money. He sold his extraordinary skills to anyone who could use them. He even used his knowledge of Classical Greek and Roman theatres to design London's first theatre for the actor James Burbage.

As Dee grew older, he was consumed by an obsession – to communicate with angels. He practised ancient incantations and stared into his crystal ball and precious antique Aztec obsidian mirror for hours on end but, try as he might, he saw no visions of angels. Help eventually came with the arrival of a young chap named Edward Kelley – a man who had lost both his ears as a punishment for 'coining', the crime of forging coins. He turned out to be an ace at seeing angels in the mirror, so they agreed that he would work for Dee on a handsome wage and wear a hat at all times to hide his lack of ears. They set off immediately in search of a foreign court where their quest would be more generously sponsored than at home.

Dee, his new young wife and children, along with Kelley and

his wife, found themselves, like many other spiritual seekers, drawn to Europe's capital of out-there mystical enquiry, Prague. Here, at the palace of the highly eccentric Holy Roman Emperor Rudolf II, they were lavishly encouraged to transcribe hours of opaque messages from an angel called Uriel and in their spare time to practise alchemy (the quest to turn base metal into gold).

Rudolf seemed to be more impressed with Kelley than with Dee and thought that limitless amounts of gold were just around the corner. He granted Kelley a tract of land and knighted him, leaving Dee increasingly dejected.

Then Kelley dropped a bombshell. He told Dee the angel Madimi had given strict instructions that Dee and Kelley should share their wives. Dee was 60 years old at the time and his wife Jane was 32. Dee reluctantly broke the news to her that night, and his diary records that she cried for a full 15 minutes before giving in. The arrangement doesn't seem to have lasted long, though. Leaving Kelley to further his fortune in Prague, Dee and his wife went home penniless to Mortlake to find that his library had been ransacked.

Elizabeth took pity on Dee and made him warden of Christ's College, Manchester. But by the time he retired, however, King James was on the throne and James hated anything that smacked of the supernatural. He spurned Dee, who died in poverty at the age of 81, bitter and unfulfilled.

It might have comforted Dee to know that Shakespeare in all likelihood based the character of Prospero in *The Tempest* on him and helped keep his memory alive long enough for later historians to record the life of this great man. *RT*

5:04

WILHELM REICH

Godfather of the sexual revolution

In 1985, the English singer-songwriter Kate Bush released the single 'Cloudbusting'. The song opens with driving strings and a curious lyric, 'I still dream of orgonon'. The accompanying video was equally strange – it starred Donald Sutherland as a heretical scientist and Kate, as his son, hauling a giant cloud-seeding machine up a hill. At the top, while Sutherland is fiddling with its pulleys and levers, boy-Kate pulls something from Sutherland's pocket. For a brief moment we see it is a paperback called *A Book of Dreams*. After Sutherland is taken away by sober authority figures in a car, it is left to boy-Kate to operate the 'cloudbuster' and bring on the rain.

It's doubtful that many folk would have understood the meaning of Bush's opening lyric, the presence of *The Book of Dreams* or why Sutherland was being taken away by the 'men in black'. To those in the know, however, Kate Bush was clearly a Reichian.

Born in Austria at the turn of the 19th century, Wilhelm Reich studied medicine and quickly rose through the psychoanalytical ranks to become one of Freud's star pupils. That is, until they fell out over orgasms. For Freud, the libido was an unruly beast, which needed to be diverted into 'healthier' pursuits. Reich believed the opposite, perceiving the rise of fascism in Europe in the 1920s and 1930s as a direct result of repressed sexual desire, sublimated into hatred and war.

For Reich, impotence, a lack of pleasure from sex or an inability to have an orgasm were symptoms of ill-health in need of treatment. He wanted nothing less than a sexual revolution, one which would liberate the uptight, aggressive authoritarianism of politics and the armoured proletariat, through full-body orgasm.

From the 1920s onwards, Reich travelled around Europe and Russia getting into hot water with his radical ideas. He took mobile sex clinics around cities, handed out condoms and created spaces for teenagers to explore their sexuality together in private. He advocated the legalization of homosexuality and abortions, fought against monetary dependence of women in marriages and argued that children should be raised in communities, to free them from the exclusive neurosis of their parents.

Reich's approach to psychoanalysing his patients was equally radical. He rejected the 'talking cure', having recognized that patients would sometimes lie or merely tell him what they thought he wanted to hear. For Reich, treatment had to transcend words. Perceiving trauma to be stored physically in the body as muscular tension, something he called 'character structure', Reich broke the golden rule of psychoanalysis (to never touch a patient) and developed physical manipulation techniques to enable emotional release.

Reich believed that unresolved conflict left a remnant of muscular tension; and as muscles attach to tendons, which attach to bones, the growing skeletal system of a child is influenced by the patterns of tension from unresolved conflict. As such, the psychological history of a person is present not just in the mind, as Freud and Jung believed, but in the body too. While it is now accepted that massage and yoga can spontaneously release 'trapped emotions', Reich's approach, despite being more holistic, is yet to be fully explored in modern psychoanalysis.

'Cancer and fascism are closely related. Fascism is the frenzy of sexual cripples, the swastika owes its symbolism to two bodies locked in genital embrace. It all stems from a longing for love', Dušan Makavejev, *WR: Mysteries of the Organism* (1971).

Having written books with titles such as *The Function of the Orgasm* (1927) and *The Mass Psychology of Fascism* (1933), it's no surprise that Reich was a **target for the Nazis**. Having relocated to Berlin in 1930, he fled persecution three years later and headed to Denmark. Here, his promotion of abortion and ideas around teenage sex were equally controversial. He fled from Denmark to Sweden, from Sweden to Norway and finally from Norway to the United States. Everywhere Reich went his ideas were scorned, his books banned and often burned for good measure. If Europe wasn't ready for his radicalism, he hoped that America would be.

While Reich was on a mission to bring peace and love to humanity, he was not without his flaws. He was notoriously grumpy and arrogant, held inconsistent views about homosexuality and – like Jung and Freud – had affairs with his patients. Those who worked with him often complained that it was his way or not at all. His haircut didn't do him any favours either.

By the time Reich reached America he was on the hunt for physical evidence of the orgasmic energy, which he coined orgone. For him, the level of pleasure derived from orgasm – from wildly ecstatic to non-existent – was a measure of a person's orgone levels, also reflected in their vitality. Those who displayed boundless energy and drive (such as Buckminster Fuller - see Chapter 4) would be considered full to the brim with orgone.

HOW TO MEASURE ORGASMIC ENERGY

Reich founded the Orgone Institute in 1942, by which time he believed he had physical evidence of orgone and that it could be measured in a human with a voltmeter when he/she was going through intense emotional release. For Reich, orgone was the universal energy, the orgiastic energy that gave birth to the universe. And while he wasn't the first to believe in an all-pervading universal energy – to the yogis it's *prana*, to the Chinese it's *chi*, for modern science it's dark matter – Reich was the first to claim this energy could be measured and seen (it was blue, apparently).

To stimulate orgone energy in the individual, Reich invented the **Orgone Energy Accumulator**. Looking like a one-person sauna, it was an upright rectangular box made of different layers of wood and metal to amplify the 'orgone energy' for any user sitting inside, rather like heat in a greenhouse. Claims around the properties of this device ranged from boosting the immune system and destruction of cancerous cells to 'orgiastic potency'.

Reich's next invention was the cloudbuster. While best known for seeding clouds, its principal function was to harness orgone energy in the atmosphere and to zap 'bad' orgone energy, which Reich believed was being emitted from the exhaust pipes of UFOs. It's fair to say at this point that Reich's own traumas were leading him towards a breakdown.

Woody Allen parodied the orgone accumulator as the orgasmatron, in his sci-fi film *Sleeper* (1973).

213

Reich's cloudbuster could supposedly produce rain by manipulating the 'orgone energy' in the atmosphere.

In relocating to America, Reich had hoped to be welcomed. His isolation and unwillingness to accept any opinion other than his own didn't win him any favours. He had become deeply paranoid, though not without reason. By the 1950s, America's own paranoia about communism led to the McCarthy witch hunts to root out the 'reds under the bed'. As a foreigner and former member of the Communist Party doing strange experiments out in the wilds of Maine, Reich was an obvious target. He was accused of running a sex racket through his sales of the Orgone Accumulator, and the US Food Administration charged him with contempt of court for violation of an obscure cosmetics labelling law.

Arguing that the judges were ill-equipped to judge his scientific inventions, Reich requested a panel of scientists but was refused. He was imprisoned for contempt of court, and his books and much of his equipment were destroyed. Twenty years after the Nazis had burned his books, American justice continued in the same vein. Reich died in prison, eight months into his sentence. Not one scientific or psychiatric journal mentioned his passing.

Wilhelm Reich dedicated his life to an exploration of the true nature of the orgasm, and a radical approach to psychoanalysis that treated both mind and body. He never stopped believing in the need for a sexual revolution. Ten years after his death, the slogan of the 1960s counterculture 'make love not war' summed up his philosophy in four words.

Over the following decades, zealous advocates of his orgone accumulator would include William Burroughs, J.D. Salinger, Allen Ginsberg, Jack Nicholson and Sean Connery. In 1973, Hawkwind sang, 'I've got an orgone accumulator, it makes me feel greater. It's a back brain stimulator,' and a young Patti Smith, working in a bookshop in Manhattan, found *The Book of Dreams*, written by Reich's son Peter, and took it home to read.

It is this book we see in Kate Bush's video for 'Cloudbusting'. The song is written from the perspective of a 12-year-old Peter growing up in Orgonon, Reich's family home in Maine, describing the tender relationship between father and son and the trauma Peter suffered in seeing his father imprisoned. 'Cloudbusting' tells the first half of Peter's story, but Patti Smith had already concluded it ten years earlier on 'Birdland', the standout track from her debut album *Horses* (1975), in which Reich, behind the controls of a UFO, returns to find his son and take him away.

While we now live in a sex-obsessed age, were he alive today Reich would doubtless feel we still have a long way to go to reach a 'full and sustained orgasmic potential'. Having dismantled the many rituals around courtship, sex is more easily obtained in Western society, but is it any better? Shame and hypocrisy around sex are still dished out daily in our tabloid newspapers with titillation on one page and a sex scandal on another. The nature of orgasm and its impacts on our health are rarely discussed. No doubt Reich would feel that there is still work to be done. DB

J.W. DUNNE

The man who experimented with time

At precisely 9pm on 7 December 1937, John William Dunne made his debut appearance on the BBC's fledgling television service, suitably attired in dinner jacket and bow tie and accompanied by a pianist. Eschewing the opportunity to belt out a cheeky ditty, Dunne chose instead to share with viewers his unique perspective on the nature of time. With the pianist's help he outlined his theory: that time isn't linear like the ascending notes on a keyboard, but a symphony of all creation in which past, present and future are intertwined. Proof of the strangeness of time and our immortality, Dunne went on to explain, can be proven using a notebook, pen and a comfy pillow.

Chances are, you've experienced the strangeness of time yourself. Let's say, for argument's sake, you're on holiday in Yorkshire for the first time and see a sign for the Rotherham Spoon Museum. Excitedly you pay your £3 and enter the building. As you do, the curator steps forward and discreetly informs you that your flies are undone. Zipping up your trousers you feel the hairs rise on the back of your neck. This whole scenario, unlikely as it seems, feels uncannily familiar as if it's happened to you before. Don't worry, you're not losing your marbles – you've just experienced déjà vu, something that most people experience at some point in their lives. And while science attempts to brush off déjà vu as an anomaly of memory, back in the early 20th century one man saw it as evidence that time is even more mysterious than Einstein dared suppose.

J.W. Dunne was born into an aristocratic Irish family in the late 19th century. An engineer who fought in the Second Boer and First World War, he earned a reputation as an aviation celebrity, flying over the Channel and designing the first British military plane. Such was the success of his aeronautical patents

Before turning his attention to time travel, Dunne was a pioneering aeroplane designer and also invented realistic artificial fishing flies.

that Dunne become a man of leisure at a young age. He wrote several books for children and another on his passion for fly-fishing. But it was the exploration of time that would eventually come to define Dunne's life and work.

In 1900, recovering in hospital from typhoid, Dunne began to experience vivid precognitive dreams. Global disasters that he'd read about in the morning papers appeared to have a surprising similarity to recent dreams. At first, he put his precognitive dreams down to a 'fault in his reality' but their regularity led to his decision to approach this with a pragmatic, scientific mind. Every morning Dunne transcribed his dreams and began to study them. After a while a pattern emerged; his dreams seemed to consist of past and future events in equal measure. Extending the experiment, Dunne enlisted the help of friends and colleagues who also began to record their dreams and look for anomalies.

For Dunne, the evidence soon became overwhelming: our dreams are composed of both past and future experiences. He formulated a philosophy – serialism – in which he proposed that time is a mentally imposed barrier by our waking consciousness. When in altered states of mind, however, it stretches out before us. Anyone who has experimented with **psychedelics** will not only recall becoming mesmerized by the patterns in the carpet but also the lengthening of time. And while Dunne never donned a kaftan and nibbled on fly agaric, he would undoubtedly have found that

Aldous Huxley's *Doors of Perception* (1954) is a good starting point for reading about the strange effects psychedelics have on our experience of time.

217

psychedelic experience supported his theory that we inhabit two separate planes of existence.

In 1927, Dunne published his most famous book, *An Experiment with Time*. At heart, he was an engineer and pragmatist, and in the introduction he expresses his disdain for both the occult sciences and Freudian psychoanalysis. For Dunne, dreams were not merely an expression of repressed sexual desire but an experience of the eternal. In our sleep, Dunne writes, released from 'Serial Time', we experience the universe as a timeless present, hence our ability to have dreams that would be considered future events in our waking state.

In *An Experiment with Time*, Dunne notes that his precognitive dreams, though uncannily similar to future events, were never exactly the same. While some could use this as an argument against Dunne – that when looking for connections we inevitably find them – the psychologist Carl Jung would have seen the minor discrepancies between Dunne's dreams and real-life events as strengthening his theory. One function of dreaming, according to Jung, is to mythologize our experiences – we retell a story or event to serve our own needs. If we can all have precognitive dreams, as Dunne believed, like all dreams they come with a twist.

TICKET TO AN IMMORTAL REALM

An Experiment with Time, much of which is autobiographical, remains a fascinating read. Some chapters, however, are muddied with mathematical formulas and convoluted phrases such as 'infinite regress', 'retro-causality' and 'quantum-interconnectedness'. Thankfully, you can skip these without missing any of the good stuff.

As well as suggesting that déjà vu gives a feeling of familiarity because we have dreamed it before, Dunne also believed that his theory offered proof of an immortal realm – one that is entered nightly when we sleep and in which we continue to exist when our bodies die. Dreams, Dunne noted, are self-illuminated; they are massless worlds without shadows in which we are unaware of the presence of our bodies. Current scientific understanding perceives photons as massless, self-illuminated and – in travelling at the speed of light – 'experiencing' past, present and future instantaneously. When the occultist Aleister

Crowley (see later in this chapter) wrote, 'I believe in the company of stars of whose fire we are created, and to which we shall return,' did he mean it literally?

Dunne died in 1949 and, for a while at least, his ideas lived on. T.S. Eliot, C.S. Lewis, Jorge Luis Borges, Aldous Huxley, William Burroughs, H.G. Wells and Graham Greene all cited Dunne as an influence on their work. J.R.R. Tolkien's unpublished novel *The Notion Club Papers* was written as a direct response to many of Dunne's ideas, as was J.B. Priestley's play *Time and the Conways*. A proper fanboy, Priestley once invited Dunne to brief his cast before the first night of a new run of his play.

After Dunne's death in 1949, Priestley continued the investigation into time, appearing in 1963 on the BBC's programme *Monitor* to appeal for letters explaining experiences of precognition from viewers for his next book, *Man and Time*.

Nowadays, the thought of discussing Einstein and Dunne in the same breath may seem ridiculous to many in the scientific arena. But it's worth remembering that why and how we dream remains a mystery. The subjective nature of dreaming means where we go at night may forever remain open to wild speculation and theories. And while Dunne's ideas can be neither proven nor disproven scientifically, you can try out his experiments. Who knows, as you hold this book and read these words for the first time, you may be feeling the hairs on the back of your neck stand up as you're overcome with the uncanny sensation that this has all happened before... DB

HOW TO CONDUCT YOUR OWN TIME EXPERIMENTS

1   Keep a notebook and pencil under your pillow.
2   On waking, remain in the same position you slept in and write down everything you can remember.
3   Keep alert for evidence of dreams in the real world.
4   Be vigilant when making any changes in your life: new situations prompt strange dreams.

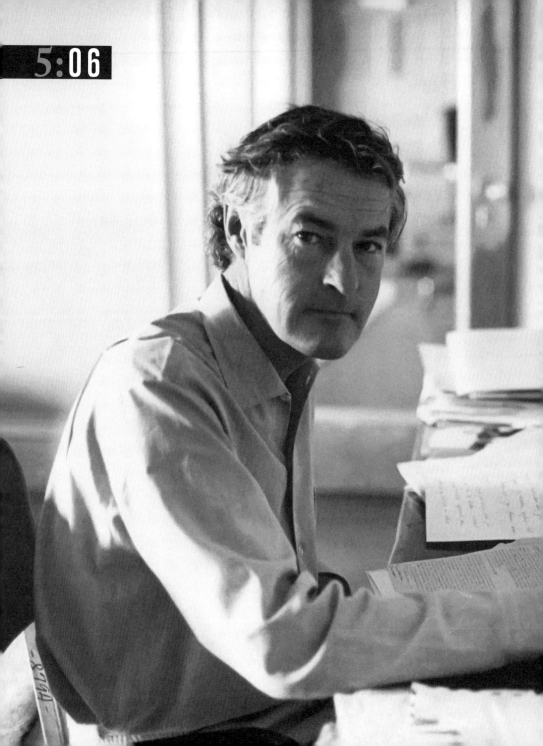
5:06

TIMOTHY LEARY

The most dangerous man in America

In the early 1960s, Timothy Leary was a lecturer in clinical psychology at Harvard University. He began to actively promote use of the psychedelic drug LSD to the general population, in the belief that this would make the world a better place. Millions upon millions of people followed his advice and as a result Leary became, in the opinion of the Nixon administration, the most dangerous man in America.

To the psychedelic community, Leary is a divisive and toxic figure who can be blamed for the negative opinion the wider population has about LSD enthusiasts. Psychedelic research, this argument goes, would be a perfectly respectable field of study had it not been for this overly messianic, irresponsible charlatan who was single-handedly responsible for legal prohibition. Others argue that the impact of the wave of psychedelic use he triggered helped create the personal computer industry and the environmental movement, and that he made more people happy than anyone else in history. These extremes of opinion, it's worth noting, are not mutually exclusive.

Leary's interest in psychedelics started when he experimented with psilocybin mushrooms during a holiday in Mexico in 1960. As he later said about the experience, during those four hours by the pool he 'learned more about the mind, the brain and its structures than in the preceding 15 years as a diligent psychologist' (Timothy Leary, *Flashbacks* (1983)). Psychedelic drugs, then largely unknown and unstudied by science, seemed to him to be a tool that would revolutionize psychology to the extent that the telescope transformed astronomy. His particular interest was in behaviour modification, and in using psychedelics to change the way patients viewed the world.

But what was the best way to promote awareness of psychedelics? Leary took advice from two prominent writers. Aldous Huxley told him that mass uptake of the drug would be dangerous and unpredictable and that he should tread cautiously, introducing the drug initially only to artists and scientists. Allen Ginsberg, in contrast, reminded Leary that they were Americans, and democrats. They couldn't keep the drug among the elites; it had to be spread widely, to everyone. Huxley died in 1963 and his influence on Leary waned, but it was only after the United States made LSD illegal, on 6 October 1966, that Leary fully dedicated himself to Ginsberg's path. In January 1967, speaking to a crowd of young people in Golden Gate Park, San Francisco, Leary told them to 'tune in, turn on and drop out'. His earlier measured caution was behind him. He was going all out to promote drug use.

AMERICA'S MOST WANTED

From this point on, Leary's life became so insanely complicated and dramatic that all we can do is soberly note the key points. He became a figurehead of the 1960s youth movement, and a friend of John Lennon and many other notable cultural figures. While attempting to run against Ronald Reagan for Governor of California, Leary was sentenced to 20 years' imprisonment for possession of a tiny amount of marijuana.

Once inside, Leary was given the standard prison psychological evaluation test – which just happened to be based, in part, on his work. Knowing what personality traits each question was assessing, he completed his questionnaire in a manner that painted him as compliant and meek, with a healthy interest in gardening. He was in no way an escape risk, or so the paperwork said, so he was placed in a minimum security prison. He escaped a few months later by pulling himself along a telephone wire that went over the fence.

He and his wife were then smuggled out of the country, for a fee of $25,000, by the domestic terrorist organization The Weather Underground. He fled to Algeria seeking the protection of the Black Panther Party who, through a strange quirk of history, were at the time viewed by the Algerian government as the official representatives of the United States. This did not go well, and the Learys were held under house arrest until they could regain their passports and escape from the Black Panthers. They fled to Switzerland, where they met an exiled French arms dealer, who offered his protection in return for the rights to Leary's future books. While briefly imprisoned in Switzerland, Leary was able to escape another prison by means of a fake heart attack and a compliant doctor.

During this time the American government were so eager to recapture Leary they placed a $5,000,000 bounty on his head. Being a globally famous wanted fugitive is stressful at the best of times, but to be one while constantly under the influence of psychedelics was in a whole new league.

On 12 September 1970, Timothy Leary escaped from a Californian jail by pulling himself along a telephone wire.

Eventually, Leary was captured in Kabul, Afghanistan, and returned to American captivity. He was placed in a cell next to Charles Manson, for a time, in the maximum-security Folsom State Prison. The FBI spread the word that he was collaborating, moving him between prisons under the alias Charlie Thrush to indicate he was a 'songbird' who was ratting on all his previous counterculture friends. To the coke-addled and paranoid 1970s counterculture, this seemed entirely plausible, and Leary was denounced by many of his former friends and colleagues – including Ginsberg. His credibility never recovered, despite his insistence that he was only pretending to collaborate in an effort to talk his way out of prison. His explanation seems plausible, for no trials or arrests resulted from information coming from Leary.

TRUTH IS IN THE EYE OF THE BEHOLDER

Leary gave Western culture a context with which to appreciate expanded awareness, which it had previously lacked. In historical accounts of people in Britain accidentally consuming psychedelic mushrooms, for example, the experience is always viewed with horror. People thought that they had lost their sanity or had been possessed by the Devil. It was Leary, with his respectable Harvard background, who framed this experience as a beneficial one, leading to wisdom and personal growth.

He was also the first to explain how 'set and setting', your mental state and surroundings, could influence the psychedelic experience in a negative or a positive way. He gave us the concept of 'reality tunnels', one of the most useful nuggets of 1960s thought (see the next section in this chapter). A reality tunnel, Leary explained, was not reality itself. It was what we think reality is. Although we think we perceive reality clearly – in fact we live inside a model of it, one of our own creation. Like all models, it is a simpler and smaller approximation that is not entirely accurate in all respects. Psychedelic drugs showed clearly how arbitrary those models were.

Leary went further. We are each responsible for our own reality tunnel, he argued. If we want to change our attitudes, behaviour, friends and beliefs, then we can. If we want to change our emotions, perception and mode of thinking then that's possible too. When others viewed Leary in a negative or positive light, he believed that was their choice, and that it said as much about them as it did about him.

'You get the Timothy Leary you deserve,' he once remarked, and if any sentence can stand as an overall judgement on his life, then it is that. JH

ROBERT ANTON WILSON

The man who didn't believe in anything

'I don't believe anything,' Robert Anton Wilson once said.
Or, at least, he tried his hardest not to. He didn't believe that
the sun would rise in the morning. He just thought that it
was incredibly likely, because all our physical sciences pointed
to it being inevitable and he wasn't aware of any evidence to
the contrary. The notion that he was right about everything,
however, and that all his prejudices and preferences were
justified, seemed to him to be on far shakier ground.

Belief is incredibly seductive, and not believing anything is
practically impossible, but no one made a better job of escaping
from it than Wilson did. As he saw it, convictions create convicts;
what you believe imprisons you, and it is just as important not to
fall for your own belief system as it is not to fall for anyone else's.

Wilson was born in Brooklyn in 1932, at the height of the Great
Depression. He contracted polio as a child and his parents were
told that he would never walk again. In desperation, they found
a doctor who agreed to treat him with the controversial Sister
Kenny method. Sister Kenny was an Australian nurse who was,
in the words of the American Medical Association, an 'ignorant
quack seeking money for her own gain'. Kenny's methods, the
medical profession insisted, simply didn't work. Nevertheless,
they worked on Wilson, and he was able to walk again.

All this had quite an impact on Wilson's thought. Every time
he took a step on his now-working legs he had good reason not
to automatically accept the establishment perspective. A period
as a devout Catholic and a period as a Marxist followed and,
after he had rejected both of those belief systems, he began to
recognize just how seductive belief systems could be. He became
fascinated by 'reality tunnels', which was a term invented by his

friend Timothy Leary. A reality tunnel is the model of reality that you construct in your brain, through years of experience and learning. Your reality tunnel is not reality itself, but what you think reality is. It is a model that we use to make sense of the world around us – but a model is by definition a smaller, simplified version of what it represents. It is not accurate in every detail. Leary and Wilson realized that we live in our reality tunnels more than we live in reality itself, and as a consequence we fail to notice when our model doesn't match the outer world. We are a species hard-wired to live in its own delusions.

The fact that we all have our own different individual reality tunnels leads to conflict and argument. There are seven billion people alive at the moment, but it is not possible to find someone who sees the world in the same way as you do, and agrees with you on every detail. To avoid the cognitive dissonance this brings, groups adopt shared reality tunnels such as Marxism, Catholicism or materialism. These are systems of thought that promise to make sense of the whole world, provided you believe them unconditionally. In the wake of Wilson's early medical, religious and political experiences, he came to define belief systems such as these as 'self-referential reality tunnels'.

In the late 1960s, Wilson was editing the letters pages of *Playboy* magazine and became increasingly fascinated by the **strange and contradictory** conspiracy-tinged letters he received. Along with his friend and colleague Robert Shea he co-wrote *The Illuminatus! Triology* (1975) – a lengthy counterculture novel that owed as much to James Joyce as it did to *Looney Tunes*. The novel grew out of the question, 'What would the world be like if all the conspiracy stories were true?' The aim of the book, according to Wilson, was to do to the state what Voltaire had done to the church.

BEYONCÉ AND THE EYE OF PROVIDENCE

The Illuminatus! Trilogy quickly became a cult classic and the ideas within it seeded themselves throughout wider culture. The idea that the 'Illuminati' was not a historical curiosity but an organization that actually existed, had members and was secretly in control of the world, comes from this book. In the decades following the book's publication, it spread from Wilson's and Shea's work to the role-playing game community,

Wilson was one of the most important figures in Discordianism, a religion based on the worship of Eris, Greek goddess of chaos and confusion. One of its tenets is 'We Discordians should split apart', so Discordianism actively encourages schisms among its followers. There has been much debate about whether Discordianism is an elaborate joke disguised as a sincere religion, or a sincere religion disguised as an elaborate joke. Most Discordians see no discrepancy between the two positions, and accept them both equally.

to video games and rap artists, and became a now all-pervasive **millennial meme**. Like much of Wilson's wider cultural impact, it was a joke that got out of hand.

Wilson quit his comfortable, well-paid *Playboy* job to become what his friend Timothy Leary called 'that most recklessly heroic person – the self-employed intellectual'. The second half of his life was financially precarious, and not without more than its fair share of tragedy, but it produced a body of work that undoubtedly raised Wilson to the position of one of the 20th century's most lucid philosophers. He wrote around 35 books, both fiction and non-fiction, through which he explored a philosophy called 'multiple-model agnosticism'.

Wilson trained his readers to no longer assume that reality was an absolute, singular thing, but instead something that we could know only as plural and subjective. He was a stubbornly 20th-century thinker, whose influences included James Joyce, Ezra Pound, Albert Einstein, Alfred Korzybski, Erwin Schrödinger and Aleister Crowley. Wilson knew that the uncertain, postmodern world revealed by the great advances of that century was frequently dismissed by those who disliked those conclusions, but he also knew that just because you wanted the comfort of absolute certainty, did not mean it existed.

THE 23 ENIGMA

Above everything, Robert Anton Wilson was a very funny writer. With his ability to make sense of chaos, the big-hearted pleasure he took in life, and his inability to take himself too seriously, he was a figure much loved by those who knew his work. Towards the end of his life he suffered from post-polio syndrome, and lacked the ability to pay for care. When word got out that he could not afford to die at home, as he wished, his readers around the world began sending him money – **typically $23 at a time**. Tens of thousands of dollars arrived in a matter of days, echoing the climax to the film *It's A Wonderful Life*, and Wilson was able to end his days in his own house. Wilson's work is currently being republished. It is recommended to anyone psychologically prepared to see the flaws in their current belief system. *JH*

The 23 enigma is the belief that most incidents and events are directly connected to the number 23, explored in *The Illuminatus! Trilogy*. In Wilson's various works, the number 23 may be considered lucky, unlucky, sinister, strange or sacred.

SEVEN WILSONIAN EXERCISES TO FLIP YOUR REALITY

Robert Anton Wilson set his readers exercises that, he claimed, would help them recognize the arbitrary nature of their reality tunnels.

1   For a week swap Facebook accounts with someone you trust. How does it change your sense of identity?

2   Spend one Sunday watching wildlife documentaries on TV. The next day at work observe the primate pack hierarchy carefully, like a scientist.

3   Start collecting evidence that 23 is a magical number. What different answers can you deduce from your evidence?

4   Try living for a week believing that everybody likes you and is trying to help you achieve your goals, and see what happens.

5   You are not allowed to say 'I' for ten days. Each time you forget, bite your thumb. Observe how this exercise changes your sense of certainty.

6   Pretend you are skilled in fortune-telling through reading tea leaves. Offer readings to friends and strangers. Observe how it alters your sense of empathy and powers of deception

7   Spend a month only reading magazines, newspapers, books, websites and blogs that subscribe to a political point of view contrary to your own.

JOSEPH CAMPBELL

The myth man

In 1929, Joseph Campbell, an academic, semi-professional athlete and jazz musician, moved into a rented shack in Woodstock, New York with an inordinately large pile of books and some sandwiches. Campbell, who was fluent in German, French and Sanskrit and already had a BA in English literature and an MA in mediaeval literature, had a voracious appetite for knowledge. Having abandoned his PhD and the constraints of academia, Campbell decided to read everything that fascinated him. This, he knew, was going to take a little time.

Once settled in his shack, Campbell divided each day into four-hour segments with a total of nine hours put aside each day for reading. He began by devouring the complete works of Plato, Freud, Thomas Mann, Jung and James Joyce. He studied the major religious tomes, the great works of fiction, read up on world mythology and dipped into Shakespeare for light relief. This he did in relative isolation for four years, clocking up an impressive 11,000-plus hours of reading time (though it's possible he may have slacked off on the odd day). The more he read, the more Campbell began to perceive curious patterns emerging out of the world's great myths and stories.

'Sit in a room and read – and read and read. And read the right books by the right people. Your mind is brought on to that level, and you have a nice, mild, slow-burning rapture all the time.' –Joseph Campbell, *The Power of Myth* (1988)

Campbell finally left his cabin for a teaching post. Not one to do things by halves, he would remain in the same job for the next 38 years. Free to lecture on his favourite subjects, Campbell began to share some of his discoveries with his students. He had come to realize that many of the key stories in the Bible – the Garden of Eden, Great Flood and Resurrection – were far from unique; variations of these stories had been told by disparate cultures across the globe, many pre-dating the Bible. For Campbell, the evidence was irrefutable; these were not historical accounts but shared myths, stories that welled up from what Jung described as our 'collective unconscious'.

Focusing his attention on the world's great legends, fairy tales and works of fiction, Campbell found another curiosity – they were nearly always variations of the same story, a monomyth that he called the 'hero's journey'. Whether it was *Ulysses, Jack and the Beanstalk, The Hobbit* or *Great Expectations*, these stories followed the same trajectory: a humble individual undergoes a difficult trial, meets a strange but helpful character, accomplishes an arduous task and returns home a changed man/woman/hobbit.

Campbell came to realize that humanity had been telling itself this same tale a thousand ways over the millennia. Why? It is a story that guides us through some of the great changes in life such as love, loss and the transition from adolescence to adulthood.

'The basic motif of the hero journey is a death and rebirth. It is an initiation ritual, leaving one condition for another and returning more mature.' –*The Power of Myth* (1988)

For Campbell, science could demonstrate how the world works; myths were there to teach us how to live in the world.

> 'Our life evokes our character. You find out about yourself as you go on; your preferred career, your nature. If a person doesn't listen to the demands of his own heart and insists on a different program you get a crack-up. The world is full of people who've stopped listening to themselves. We need myths to put us back in our centre. Myths are much more important and true than history. History is just journalism and you know how reliable that is.'
> –*The Power of Myth* (1988)

After committing his ideas to print in *The Hero with a Thousand Faces* (1949), Campbell began to garner support. Befriended by George Lucas, Campbell played a crucial role in shaping the narrative of *Star Wars*, which closely followed his 12 stages of the hero's journey. The dark woods and unchartered oceans of old legends were replaced with outer space; the supernatural aid came in the form of Obi-Wan Kenobi and a couple of camp robots; reaching the 'threshold' was the bar scene, where Luke is in unfamiliar territory and already out of his depth when a bog-eyed walrus and pig-nosed-melty-face start getting shirty with him; Obi-Wan Kenobi, his supernatural aid, comes to his rescue.

Star Wars became an unprecedented global phenomenon. Had he lived to see its continuing popularity in the 21st century, Campbell would have taken this as even greater proof of our hunger for modern variations of the monomyth. Once you know it, you'll be able to spot the hero's journey everywhere, from the books of J.K. Rowling and Dan Brown to *Indiana Jones* and *The Matrix*.

For Hollywood, Campbell was both a blessing and curse. Script writers finally had a formula that had proven success. For a while, cinema became saturated with films about the lone, struggling male hero. But Campbell never claimed the hero's journey was the only story – rather that, for our patriarchal past, it was the big one.

Campbell believed that 'Myth evolves as culture evolves'. Matching our great societal shifts in the past hundred years, the 20th and 21st century have seen an evolution in myths, with the rise of the anti-hero, more female-driven narratives and complex family sagas (epitomized by the popularity of the box set).

A DIVISIVE MYTHIC MESSAGE

Campbell ultimately came to view all definitions of God as metaphorical, which deeply irritated theists. He also put great value on religious myths and rituals, which got up the noses of atheists.

> 'Half the people in the world think that the metaphors of their religious traditions are facts. And the other half contends that they are not facts at all. As a result we have people who consider themselves believers because they accept metaphors as facts, and we have others who classify themselves as atheists because they think religious metaphors are lies. All religions are true but none are literal.'
> —*The Power of Myth* (1988)

Just for good measure, Campbell annoyed academics too, who viewed him as a populist. Ironically, his most famous book, *The Hero with a Thousand Faces*, first published in 1949, now feels overly academic. Campbell is best enjoyed in interviews and lectures, in which his joy and passion are infectious.

A six-part TV series *Power of Myth*, broadcast in 1988 (a year after Campbell's death), made him an almost household name in the United States. No mean feat, considering it is essentially just Campbell in conversation for six hours, discussing mythology. It was his avuncular manner and illuminating responses that delighted audiences. When confronted with the big questions – the kind that leave most philosophers clearing their throats or spouting psychobabble – Campbell's responses were lucid, thoughtful and satisfying. He was able to relate his subject matter to our everyday concerns and, unlike most philosophers, living or dead, appeared to have life figured out and was content.

> 'As you proceed through life, following your own path, birds will shit on you. Don't bother to brush it off. Getting a comedic view of your situation gives you spiritual distance. Having a sense of humour saves you.'
> —Diane K. Osbon, *A Joseph Campbell Companion* (1995)

In summing up the secret of a good life, Campbell was fond of saying, 'Follow your bliss.' It might sound dangerously like some saccharine New Age mantra, but for Campbell it was key to a happy life. For those of us who yearn for adventure, wish they had a more fulfilling job, crave the opportunity to love or be loved, 'follow your bliss' is the call to the hero within. It is the path that many of those featured in this book have taken, risking the pitfalls and potential failures of what lay ahead. Whether it's the story of Buddha, Bilbo or Buffy, myths are there to help us challenge expectations and convention and take a leap of faith into the unknown, as countless have done before us – and, in doing so, begin our own hero's journey.

'If you do follow your bliss you put yourself on a kind of track that has been there all the while, waiting for you, and the life that you ought to be living is the one you are living. Don't be afraid; doors will open where you didn't know they were going to be.' DB

TWELVE STEPS OF SKYWALKER'S JOURNEY

1   **Ordinary world:** Luke is on the farm.
2   **Call to adventure:** Luke buys a couple of camp robots and gets a strange message from a princess.
3   **Refusal of the call:** Luke feels duty bound to stick around for the new lambing season.
4   **Meeting with the mentor:** Luke meets Sir Alec Guinness.
5   **Crossing the threshold:** Luke visits a dodgy pub with Sir Alec Guinness and incites a bar brawl.
6   **Tests, allies, enemies:** Luke gets to grips with his lightsaber and travels to the Death Star.
7   **The approach (meeting with the goddess):** Luke meets the princess. Not knowing it's his sister, he gets the hots for her.
8   **The belly of the whale:** Luke and the gang slip down the garbage shoot and all seems lost.
9   **The ordeal:** It's the big one – Luke must destroy the Death Star before teatime.
10 **Rescue from without:** Luke is saved by Han, while Sir Alec Guinness helps him destroy the Death Star from beyond the grave.
11 **Return with the elixir:** Luke and pals return to the rebel base feeling pretty smug.
12 **The reward:** Luke has saved the day and is honoured; C-3PO gets a good polishing.

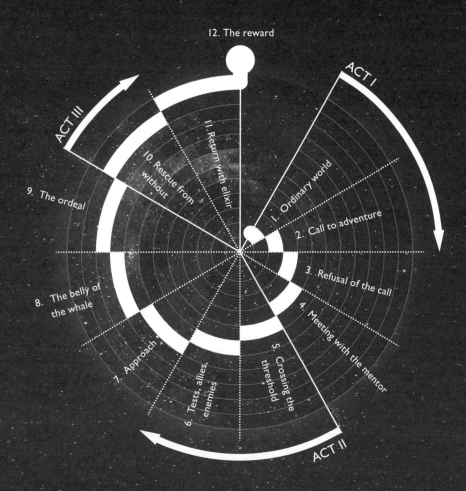

12. The reward

ACT I

ACT III

11. Return with elixir

10. Rescue from without

9. The ordeal

1. Ordinary world

2. Call to adventure

3. Refusal of the call

4. Meeting with the mentor

8. The belly of the whale

5. Crossing the threshold

7. Approach

6. Tests, allies, enemies

ACT II

The Twelve Steps of a
HERO'S JOURNEY

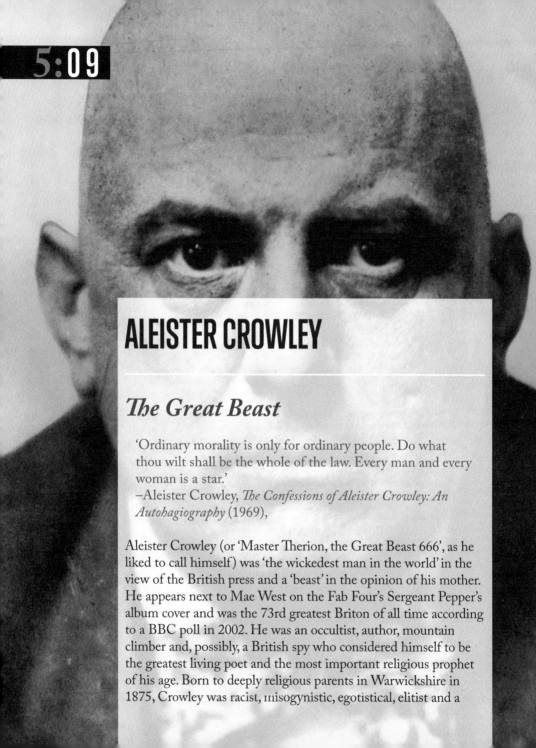

ALEISTER CROWLEY

The Great Beast

'Ordinary morality is only for ordinary people. Do what thou wilt shall be the whole of the law. Every man and every woman is a star.'
–Aleister Crowley, *The Confessions of Aleister Crowley: An Autohagiography* (1969),

Aleister Crowley (or 'Master Therion, the Great Beast 666', as he liked to call himself) was 'the wickedest man in the world' in the view of the British press and a 'beast' in the opinion of his mother. He appears next to Mae West on the Fab Four's Sergeant Pepper's album cover and was the 73rd greatest Briton of all time according to a BBC poll in 2002. He was an occultist, author, mountain climber and, possibly, a British spy who considered himself to be the greatest living poet and the most important religious prophet of his age. Born to deeply religious parents in Warwickshire in 1875, Crowley was racist, misogynistic, egotistical, elitist and a major arsehole – but he was also arguably the most influential figure in the spiritual evolution of the 20th century.

Crowley had a privileged Victorian upbringing and inherited a sizeable portion of the family wealth at the age of 11, after his father died of cancer. A series of expulsions from a number of public schools followed and he left Cambridge University at the age of 23, without a degree, having written a collection of erotic poetry called *White Stains* (1898). This was deemed obscene, and had to be published abroad. By this time, Crowley had already strongly rejected his pious Christian upbringing and developed his life-long interest in sex, magic and the purposeful derangement of the senses.

Crowley began his study of ritual magic in earnest and was initiated into the influential occult group the Outer Order of the Golden Dawn, in 1898. The following year he bought Boleskine House, by Loch Ness in Scotland, in order to perform a lengthy magical working. This took many months and involved summoning and binding the 12 Dukes and Kings of Hell, in order to gain an audience with his Holy Guardian Angel.

He abandoned the ritual early and it is said he failed to properly banish the spirits he summoned. Boleskine has had a dark reputation in paranormal circles ever since, and a later owner committed suicide at the house. In 1970, the property was bought by Led Zeppelin's Jimmy Page, a major Crowley aficionado, and it was badly damaged in a fire in 2015.

Crowley finally encountered his Holy Guardian Angel – or at least an entity named Aiwass he later described as such – in Cairo in 1904. Crowley's wife, Rose, had become delirious, and told her husband that the falcon-headed Egyptian god Horus wished to contact him. Crowley wasn't convinced that his wife even knew who Horus was, so he took her to the Cairo museum and challenged her to locate him. Rose wandered past several obvious representations of the god, to Crowley's smug amusement, before pointing to an otherwise unremarkable wooden painting and proclaiming, 'There he is!'

The wooden stele did indeed include a form of the god Horus, but what struck Crowley was the museum's catalogue number for the piece: 666. This number, well known as the number of the Beast to all biblical scholars and Iron Maiden fans, was the number he used to refer to himself. Startled by this spooky synchronicity, he dutifully obeyed the strange instructions that his wife was receiving.

Following Rose's instructions, he retreated to their drawing room, which was arranged into a sparse temple for one hour a day starting at midday, over a period of three days. There he sat at a desk and heard the voice of Aiwass, the otherworldly entity who was acting as a minister for Horus, coming from the room behind him. Without turning to look, he dutifully wrote down everything that Aiwass dictated. The result was *The Book of the Law* (1904) – a religious text that is sparse, hypnotic, horribly beautiful and strangely frightening.

The Book of the Law became the core text in Thelema, a religion of Crowley's devising. Thelema took the religious focus away from a higher power, and centred it firmly on the individual self. Our understanding of our place in the universe was no longer that of beings subservient to a higher Lord, a saviour who offered protection but who would punish us if we didn't obey. Instead, we became the centre of our own universes, responsible for our own lives. The individual's personal will then became paramount, as made apparent in *The Book of the Law*'s most famous line: 'Do what thou wilt shall be the whole of the law.'

This was part of a larger gear change in the human story: democracy and universal suffrage were replacing emperors and tsars, Einstein's relativity was superseding Newtonian physics, and modernism was challenging the simpler perspectives of pre-20th-century art. The concept of individualism had been growing in Western culture since the Enlightenment and the English Civil War, but Crowley brought it to its bleak natural conclusion at the exact moment the world was ready for it. Individualism, as Crowley painted it, was both liberating and isolating. It rescued people from tyranny, yet caused conflict and violence. It was not 'nice' or 'good', but it was necessary.

PROPHET OF THE 20TH CENTURY

Thelema never grew into the new religious movement that Crowley dreamed of, but his influence was nevertheless profound. Gerald Gardener, the founder of Wicca and modern witchcraft, borrowed heavily from him. Crowley can be linked to Scientology, Discordianism, psychedelia and Satanism. He prepared the ground for the growth of Western interest in Eastern religion, and he

Aleister Crowley with his wife Rose and daughter Lola Zaza (1909).

is an unavoidable cornerstone for all forms of ceremonial magic and occult studies. The huge movement typically covered by the umbrella term New Age, and the **freedom to define ourselves** as 'spiritual but not religious', can be linked quite directly to his work.

Aleister Crowley died a penniless heroin addict in a Hastings boarding house in 1947. It is hard to separate the man from the dark, cruel, frightening imagery that he used very deliberately as a source of personal reputation and power and which made him such an attractive figure to rock stars such as John Lennon, David Bowie and Ozzy Osbourne. He was a hard man to like and very much the product of his age and class. Ultimately, and just like the individualism he released on society, Aleister Crowley was a man who was liberating, frightening and entirely necessary. _JH_

Crowley was a big fan of Ayn Rand, writing of her novel The Fountainhead: 'It is one of finest books I have ever read, and my friends in America insist on recognizing me in the main character.' There are indeed many similarities between Crowley's philosophy and Rand's. The fact that their ideas appeal respectively to both the counterculture and right-wing Christian America makes for a surprising example of cognitive dissonance.

ALAN WATTS

The guru who explained the unexplainable

'The meaning of life is just to be alive. It is so plain and so obvious and so simple. And yet, everybody rushes around in a great panic as if it were necessary to achieve something beyond themselves.'
–Alan Watts podcast

Alan Watts, self-styled 'genuine fake', reluctant guru and Zen scholar is more or less forgotten in Britain, the country in which he was born. He was never well known there even at his apogee, as a countercultural hero on the west coast of America in the 1960s, where he still retains a small but passionate following. The writer Aldous Huxley described him as 'a curious man; half monk and half racecourse operator', to which Watts wholeheartedly agreed. His English public-school-educated voice was rich and deep, like a prophet's, and his laugh juicy and contagious. He carried a silver cane 'for pure swank', and hung out with Ken Kesey and Jack Kerouac, though the latter didn't care for Watts, parodying him as Arthur Whale in *On the Road* (1957).

An inveterate hedonist, philanderer, sexual masochist, draft dodger, alcoholic and heavy smoker, Watts was a long way from the spiritual role models that most tend to associate with the profession of wisdom. He was married three times, fathered seven children, was condemned by his ex-wives and derided or ignored by many of his contemporaries. Those wishing to browse any of his books are usually required to enter the benighted 'spirituality', 'popular philosophy' or even 'self-help' sections of a bookshop, replete with tomes packaged in the livery of the New Age: doves in flight, setting suns, floating clouds and so on.

Even here Watts features as a marginal figure, having never achieved the prominence of Beatles' guru Maharishi Ji, Deepak

Chopra, Bhagwan Sri Rajneesh, or any of the other would-be sages who captured the imagination of the hippy generation and their inheritors. This obscurity is easily explicable. Watts' thinking was deeply watermarked with pragmatism, empiricism and common sense. He did not buy into karma, as it was popularly understood. He did not believe that there was much to be achieved by sitting cross-legged, berobed, or in meditating for hours: 'A cat sits until it is done sitting, and then gets up, stretches, and walks,' he would say. And besides, Alan Watts was a lousy name for someone offering enlightenment. It sounded more like someone involved in selling automobiles (which, in fact, his father was).

THE RELUCTANT GURU

Watts was born in 1915 in Chislehurst, on the outskirts of London. During school holidays – while he was a scholar at King's School in Cambridge – he went on trips with the Buddhism enthusiast Francis Croshaw, who first helped him develop his interest in Eastern religion. At the age of 16, Watts became secretary of the London Buddhist Lodge. By the time he was 21, he had already published his first book, *The Spirit of Zen* (1936).

That same year, Watts met the American heiress Eleanor Everett, whose mother was involved with a traditional Zen Buddhist circle in New York. They married and moved to America, where he became an Episcopal priest at a college campus.

He left for San Francisco in 1950 (his biographer, Monica Furlong, hints at indiscretions with students), separating once and for all from his Christian roots. In relocating to California, Watts found his true vocation – communicating Eastern philosophical ideas to Western audiences through books, lectures, and radio and TV appearances. He described himself as a 'spiritual entertainer' and was able to express himself with a clarity that was almost supernatural:

'I want to make one thing absolutely clear. I am not a Zen Buddhist, I am not advocating Zen Buddhism, I am not trying to convert anyone to it. I have nothing to sell. I approach you in the same spirit as a musician with his piano or a violinist with his violin. I just want you to enjoy a point of view that I enjoy.'
–Alan Watts podcast

His ability to put across complex philosophical or
psychological concepts into plain, direct language (and also
with a profound sense of fun), may have been met with caution
by academics but proved to be hugely popular with a disparate
Californian audience. Listen to any of his recorded lectures and
you can often hear sharp intakes of breath from the audience
as he treads on one taboo after another, along with gales of
laughter and Watts' own rich, baritone chuckle. When asked
who his typical audience was, he replied:

'The thoughtful person who feels uncertain of his roots; who
has seen the replacement of Faith by Reason and has learnt the
barrenness of Reason alone, whose head is satisfied but whose
heart thirsts. He has much knowledge, much education, much
power of intellect, but he finds that there is a gulf between what
he thinks and what he feels and does.'
–Alan Watts podcast

While immersed in the counterculture of the 1950s and
1960s, Watts was wary of its limitations. He found the Beats,
interpretation of Zen – as doing what you pleased – 'childish'.
His response to the proliferation of mind-expanding drugs,
which he sampled, was: 'When you've got the message, hang up
the phone.' For him, psychedelic drugs were simply instruments,
like microscopes, telescopes and telephones. 'The biologist does
not sit with eye permanently glued to the microscope, he goes
away and works on what he has seen.'

Throughout the 1960s, Watts played host to many of the
luminaries of the counterculture – Timothy Leary and Robert
Anton Wilson – on board the houseboat *Vallejo* near San Francisco.
He toured extensively, appeared on radio and lectured to every
faction of society from the hippies to the heads of IBM and the US
military. When the proliferation of fans and admirers got too much,
he would slip away to a secluded cabin in the woods to write.

Through his understanding of Zen, evil could not be destroyed
any more than good; rather they are polar opposites of the same
thing, like poles of a magnet. Destruction is as necessary as
creation. Chaos must exist if we are to know what order is. Both
aspects of reality, in tension with one another, are necessary to

keep the whole game going: the unity of opposites.

Follow this through, and this can lead to some fairly shocking moral reasoning. When the American composer and Zen follower John Cage was asked, 'Don't you think there's too much suffering in the world?', he answered, 'I think there's just the right amount.' Watts, however, was at pains to explain that this did not equate with passivity in the face of suffering. For him, Zen made no promises about happiness or the life to come, and it made no claims that the world was anything other than the one you see in front of you. It was, however, an optimistic world view, full of humour and irreverence, and deeply tolerant of human failings and flaws.

'I had a discussion with a great master in Japan, and we were talking about the various people who are working to translate the Zen books into English, and he said, "That's a waste of time. If you really understand Zen, you can use any book. You could use the Bible. You could use *Alice in Wonderland*. You could use the dictionary, because the sound of the rain needs no translation."'
–Alan Watts, *The Book: On the Taboo Against Knowing Who You Are* (1966)

TUTOR TO THE 21ST CENTURY

Although words were his tools, Watts never tired of pointing out their inadequacy. He rejoiced in his role as a communicator of ideas, even as he cast doubt on the value of ideas themselves. He would undoubtably have found the idea amusing and apposite to leave the pages about him in this book blank. After all, the Taoist philosopher Lao Tse said, 'Those that speak don't know and those who know don't speak.' But then, as Watts was fond of pointing out, Lao Tse *said that*. As Watts saw it, the world itself was fundamentally paradoxical.

Watts was prolific over his 58 years. He died in 1973 after producing 27 books and hundreds of lectures, all of which are available online. They bear intriguing titles such as 'On Being Vague', 'Death', 'Nothingness', 'The Spectrum of Love'. His books *The Meaning of Happiness* (1940), *Wisdom of Insecurity* (1951) and *The Book: On the Taboo Against Knowing Who You Are* (1966) are striking primers for his work, laying out his ideas that life has no intrinsic meaning, any more than a piece of music had an intrinsic 'point'; and that we are all as much continuous with the physical universe as a wave is continuous with the ocean.

Watts retains a hardcore of enthusiasts who 'get' his message. John Lloyd, who originated many of the great British comedy shows of the last 20 years (including *QI*) considers Watts to be the only person who ever explained the world to him and chose *The Book* as the title he would take with him onto a desert island when he appeared on BBC Radio 4's *Desert Island Discs*.

Other champions include Jarvis Cocker, Jeff Bridges, Johnny Depp and *South Park* creators Matt Stone and Trey Parker, who animated a series of his lectures. In recent years, Watts made an unlikely cameo as an app in the 2013 sci-fi film *Her*, while Cheryl Cole chose to open her 2014 album *Only Human* with a two-minute speech from Watts.

What Alan Watts taught, above all else, is that everything is transitory. Everything comes and goes. Watts himself did not exist in a perpetual state of spiritual bliss. He died an alcoholic. In his later years, he cut a Dickensian figure, working desperately to support his seven children and, presumably, his two ex-wives (by the time he died he was on a third). But he was by no account an unhappy drunk. He never expressed guilt or regret about his so-called vices, and never missed a lecture or a writing deadline.

If Watts' own example is to be taken into account, being 'enlightened' doesn't always make you happy or protect you from all of life's vicissitudes. Yet it is still something worth attaining. Why? In Watts' own words:

'There are no such things as things; that is to say separate events. There are no nouns in the physical world. If you awaken from this illusion, and you understand that black implies white, self implies other, life implies death... you can conceive yourself. Not as a stranger in the world on probation, not as something that has arrived here by fluke, but you can begin to feel your own existence as absolutely fundamental. What you are basically, deep, deep down, far, far in, is simply the fabric and structure of existence itself.' π

SEEKERS' DIRECTORY

FALCO TARASSACO

FIELD TRIP Visit Damanhur in Italy, where you can explore the Temples of Humankind, observe rituals and learn more about the Damanhurian philosophy – damanhur.org

DOCUMENTARY *The No9 Bus to Utopia*: Episode 1: 'Damanhur' (2015) – bit.ly/OdditoriumDamanhur

BOOK David Bramwell, *The No9 Bus to Utopia* (2014)

RADIO DOCUMENTARY 'Between the Ears: Time Travelling in Italy' (2013) – BBC Radio 3

AYN RAND*

ALBUM Rush, *2112* (1976)

DOCUMENTARY *All Watched over by Machines of Loving Grace* (2011), series written and directed by Adam Curtis

*Please note that the authors of this book feel unable to recommend any of Rand's actual books or her philosophy of Objectivism on moral and qualitative grounds. There are, however, some dirty rock grooves on Rush's 1976 classic Rand-inspired, *2112*, which lyrically bears an uncanny resemblance to Ben Elton's *We Will Rock You*, created in 2002. Coincidence? You decide.

JOHN DEE

FIELD TRIP Visit Dee's Obsidian Mirror at the British Museum.

PLAY William Shakespeare, *The Tempest* (1610)

BOOK Donald C. Laycock, *The Complete Enochian Dictionary: A Dictionary of the Angelic Language as Revealed to Dr. John Dee and Edward Kelley* (2001)

BOOK Philip Carr-Gomm and Richard Heygate, *The Book of English Magic* (2010)

WILHELM REICH

BOOK Robert Anton Wilson, *Wilhelm Reich in Hell* (1987)

FILM *Sleeper* (1973), directed by Woody Allen

MUSIC VIDEO Kate Bush, 'Cloudbusting' (1985)

BOOK Wilhelm Reich, *Listen, Little Man!* (1945)

FIELD TRIP The Wilhelm Reich Museum, Orgonon, Dodge Pond Road, Rangeley, Maine

BOOK Peter Reich, *A Book of Dreams* (1973)

J.W. DUNNE

ESSAY Aldous Huxley, 'The Doors of Perception' (1954)

BOOK J.W. Dunne, *An Experiment with Time* (1927)

PLAY J.B. Priestley, 'Time and the Conways' (1937)

ESSAY J.B. Priestley, 'Man and Time' (1964)

TIMOTHY LEARY

BOOK John Higgs, *I Have America Surrounded: The Life of Timothy Leary* (2006)

BOOK Timothy Leary, *The Politics of Ecstasy* (1998)

DOCUMENTARY *Dying to Know: Ram Dass and Timothy Leary* (2014)

AUTOBIOGRAPHY Timothy Leary, *Flashbacks: An Autobiography* (1983)

ROBERT ANTON WILSON

BOOK SERIES Robert Anton Wilson and Robert Shea, *The Illuminatus! Trilogy* (1975)

BOOK SERIES Robert Anton Wilson, *Cosmic Trigger Trilogy* (1977)

BOOK Robert Anton Wilson, *Prometheus Rising* (1983)

BOOK John Higgs, *The KLF: Chaos, Magic and the Band Who Burned a Million Pounds* (2013)

PLAY Daisy Eris Campbell, *Robert Anton Wilson's Cosmic Trigger* – cosmictriggerplay.com

JOSEPH CAMPBELL

BOOK/AUDIO/TV SERIES Joseph Campbell, *The Power of Myth* (1988)

FILM *Star Wars Episode IV: A New Hope* (1977)

AUDIO *The Wisdom of Joseph Campbell* (2005), Michael Toms in conversation with Joseph Campbell

ALEISTER CROWLEY

FIELD TRIP Pay a visit to Woodvale Cemetery in Brighton where Aleister Crowley was cremated.

RELIGIOUS ORGANIZATION Join Crowley's group the Ordo Templi Orientis (O.T.O.)

BOOK John Moore, *Aleister Crowley: A Modern Master* (2009)

BOOK Lawrence Sutin, *Do What Thou Wilt: A Life of Aleister Crowley* (2002)

BOOK Aleister Crowley, Rose Edith Kelly and Aiwass, *The Book of the Law* (1904)

ALAN WATTS

BOOKS Alan Watts, *The Book: On the Taboo Against Knowing Who You Are* (1966), *The Wisdom of Insecurity* (1951), *The Way of Zen* (1957)

BIOGRAPHY Monica Furlong, *Genuine Fake* (1986)

YOUTUBE ANIMATION Trey Parker and Matt Stone, *The Zen Wisdom of Alan Watts*

GIANT PUPPET A giant puppet Alan Watts talking about life – facebook.com/PuppetAlanWatts

ABOUT THE AUTHORS

DAVID BRAMWELL

David co-presents the fortnightly podcast *Odditorium* and presents and produces the *Waterfront* podcast on behalf of the Canal & River Trust. He is a regular contributor to BBC Radio 3 and Radio 4, has made programmes on Ivor Cutler and Damanhur for *Archive Hour* and *Between the Ears*, and been a guest on *The Museum of Curiosity* and *The Verb*. In 2011, he won a Sony Silver Award for his work on Radio 3's *The Haunted Moustache*.

He is the creator of the best-selling Cheeky Guides and author of two memoirs, *The No9 Bus to Utopia* (2014), ('Packed with gags, wisdom and pathos'– Tom Hodgkinson) and *The Haunted Moustache* (2016) ('Neurologically, this will light you up like a Christmas tree'– Alan Moore).

David has toured several award-winning shows and is the co-creator of *Sing-along-a-Wickerman*. He also gives entertaining lectures on topics ranging from ghost villages and time travel to postal pranks. He is, however, at his happiest performing in the back room of a pub. It is worth noting that David is a medical man by rumour only; approach with extreme caution, particularly if he offers to whip out your tonsils in exchange for a packet of biscuits.
drbramwell.com, @drbramwell

JO KEELING

A devotee to slow and thoughtful journalism, Jo is proud to be part of a growing subculture of independent publishers. She is the founder of *Ernest Journal*, a magazine for the curious and adventurous that encourages readers to slow down and appreciate simple pleasures while rekindling a thirst for knowledge and exploration.

She is also the editor of *Waterfront*, a magazine for Friends of the Canal & River Trust, which satisfies her healthy inclination towards Victorian invention and lets her geek out over river etymology and ox-bow lakes. She also curates talks and immersive experiences on the theme of water and landscape for festivals.

She co-authored *Wild Guide: Devon, Cornwall and South West* (2013), writes regularly for *Countryfile, The Simple Things, The Guardian* and *Independent*, and has spoken about independent publishing for a Guardian Masterclass and various other events.

A committed hydrophile, Jo is happiest when immersed in water, whether she's taking a cheeky dip in a London lido, seeking out hot springs or embarking on a bracing sea swim in her home town of Brighton.

slowjo.co.uk, @SlowJoKeeling

ernest.

Ernest Journal is a magazine for the curious and adventurous. It is a guide for those who appreciate true craftsmanship, who are fascinated by curious histories and who care more for timeless style than trends. Over the past three years, the journal has covered such diverse subjects as sea monsters, untranslatable words, wild man mythology, Victorian diableries, Brutalism, Iceland's Huldufólk, ghost radio stations, the abused tintype, post-apocalyptic glass making, the psychology of Antarctic exploration, cryonics in Sussex, Futurist cooking, crossmodalism, solargraphy, the vindaloo, and has visited a room filled with 900 frozen brains.
ernestjournal.co.uk

'It's hard to describe the excitement I felt when I first held a copy of *Ernest Journal*. It was as though someone had reached into the deepest recesses of my mind and turned its muddled lumber into an exquisite object. It was like that moment when you meet someone and know you'll be friends for life. I have to force myself to read it slowly. Every word, every beautiful illustration feels charged with meaning and makes me want to pull on my boots and wander off into the unknown.'
John Mitchinson, *QI*

'*Ernest Journal* is ridiculously beautiful and almost too wonderful to read. Getting the latest edition is like holding the new album from your favourite band before you've played it.'
Wolfgang Wild, *Retronaut*

Launch of the Year, Digital Magazine Awards (2014)
Shortlisted for Magpile's Best New Magazine (2014)

⊘ODITORIUM

The Odditorium podcast is a portal into the fringes of culture: its mavericks and pranksters, adventurers and occultists, artists, comics, eroticists and even the odd chef. Each episode features a guest speaker recorded before a live audience. It is ably hosted by author David Bramwell and comic actor Dave Mounfield (BBC Radio 4's *Count Arthur Strong's Radio Show*) who frame the topic with their mixture of humour, insight, silliness and an obsession with biscuits. The show is produced by Andrew Mailing and double Sony Award-winner Lance Dann, whose sound design adds an extra layer of wit and spice to the mix. The podcast broke into iTunes' top ten Arts and Culture list, has featured in *The Guardian*'s 'Top 50 Essential Podcasts' and continues to tour with live events at festivals.

The podcast features episodes on people covered in this book, including Ivor Cutler, Baroness Elsa von Freytag-Loringhoven, Ken Campbell and Francis Galton, as well as talks given by our contributors John Higgs, Sarah Angliss and James Burt.

Why does a dolphin's vagina corkscrew? What is the best song to commit suicide to? Why is a hanged man's severed hand so valuable? What is the origin of the rudest word in English? Why are we so obsessed with big willies? Subscribe to the podcast and you will find out all the answers you need, and a few you don't.

Subscribe to the *Odditorium* podcast on iTunes, Stitcher or your favourite podcatcher, oddpodcast.com

'A taste for genius matched by eccentricity'
Bella Todd, *The Guardian*

CONTRIBUTORS

SARAH ANGLISS

Sarah is a composer, performer, roboticist and sound historian. Her research interests include the use of trained songbirds as domestic music machines ('The Bird Fancyer's Delight', BBC Radio 4), ventriloquism and the uncanny (*Unheimlich Manoeuvres*, The Wire) and Britain's secret 1980s nuclear survivalists. She's currently writing an opera about Charles Byrne, the Irish giant featured in this book. **sarahangliss.com**

MARK BLACKMORE

Mark currently resides in the Falkland Islands, where he spends his time standing on cliffs looking windswept and interesting but occasionally tripping over penguins. He has written for a wide range of magazines including *BBC History, Focus, Countryfile, When Saturday Comes, Gardens Illustrated* and, of course, *Ernest Journal*.

JAMES BURT

James is a computer programmer who researches odd subjects in his spare time from ley lines to the eeriness of the Sussex landscape. James is currently working on a book about the history and culture of the British curry house. He is banned from three National Trust properties and is awaiting appeal from a fourth. **orbific.com**

TONY GILL

Tony is a teacher and performance poet, whose first collection of poems, under his *nom de plume* of Gilli Bloodaxe, was published by Matador Press. He lives in a tiny house in Gilly Gilly Ossenfeffer Katzenellen Bogen by the Sea. **gillibloodaxe.co.uk**

DIARMUID HESTER

Diarmuid was born in Kilkenny, Ireland. Failing to play the sport of hurling adequately, he was forcibly removed. He now lives in Brighton and has a PhD in literature, bringing further shame on his family. He has contributed to *LA Review of Books, Gorse Magazine* and academic journals that use the word 'pen' as a verb. **diarmuidhester.com**

JOHN HIGGS

John is the author of *Watling Street* and *Stranger Than We Can Imagine: Making Sense of the Twentieth Century*, as well as biographies of The KLF and Timothy Leary. His blood iron count is above the recommended level of 50 and currently stands at 1754. **jmrhiggs.blogspot.co.uk**

SIMON INGRAM

Simon is an author and journalist preoccupied with Britain's high places. He is the author of *Between the Sunset and the Sea: A View of 16 British Mountains* and editor of *Trail*.

EMMA KILBY

Emma combines writing with showing off, including cabaret Diva turns, psychedelic folk singing, script-writing, character comedy, theatre-making, voice-over and radio work. She is also a corporate coach and trainer. Emma has been devising a theatre show about Ayn Rand for two years, but David Hare got there before her. **emmakilbey.com**
Photo by Toby Aimes

TIM LOTT

Tim Lott was born in Southall, West London in 1956. He is a journalist and author of *The Scent of Dried Roses* and *White City Blue*, which won the Whitbread First Novel Award. It was followed by *Rumours of Hurricane* (2002), a portrait of working-class life in Britain in the 1980s, which was shortlisted for the Whitbread Novel Award. **timlottwriter.wordpress.com**

DANIEL MAIER

Daniel is a comedy writer and occasional performer, who has worked with Harry Hill, Alistair McGowan, Peter Serafinowicz, Ant & Dec and Sacha Baron Cohen and remains significantly less well known than all of them. He has put together a compilation of songs covered by The Fall and written two episodes of *Emmerdale*, making him possibly Britain's least prolific soap writer. **@danielmaier**

SIR TIM SMIT

Things that led Tim to where he is now: a cloudburst, sheltering in an estate agents, a reckless gamble, emigration to Cornwall, the gift of a pig, hot coffee and sensitive lips, a dormant degree in archaeology and driving to the first roundabout in Cornwall at sunset where a spoil heap turned ochrous red and he imagined a world of lost civilizations in the crater of a volcano. He's made records, books and mistakes and turned them into the life he knows now.

RICHARD TURNER

Richard has avoided working for a living for most of his life by acting, writing, script-editing then creating and producing just one radio programme: *The Museum of Curiosity*. He has three claims to fame: he co-wrote the poem 'What Are You, Theatre?' with Rik Mayall, he gave the phrase 'International Man of Mystery' to Austin Powers and has the world's oldest mobile voicemail outgoing message, unchanged since 1994.

ABIGAIL WHYTE

Abigail is a writer based in the Wye Valley. A perpetual student, forager, cross-country runner, cyclist and mother, Abigail will one day ignore all other distractions, sit down and push out the novel bouncing around in her head. Just not yet. **abigailwhyte.com**

ACKNOWLEDGEMENTS

The authors would like to extend thanks to: Ken McNaught, Tim Hunkin, Eleanor and Sandy from Vanishing Point, Jeremy Cutler, John Tingey, Daisy Campbell and the 'Ken Campbell Changed My Life' Facebook group, Russell Rose, Emma Hiwaizi, the Buckminster Fuller Institute and the Cosanti Foundation as well as Tigrilla and Bertuccia at Damanhur. With particular thanks to our publishing team at Hodder & Stoughton: Jonathan Shipley, Iain Campbell and Antonia Maxwell, and Lance Dann, Andrew Mailing and Dave Mounfield from *Odditorium* podcast. Finally Tina Smith, Abigail Whyte, Sam Young, Mark Blackmore and all of the *Ernest Journal* team - thank you!

PHOTO CREDITS